AF333265

BROADGATE

Paintings and Drawings
1989-1990
by

Robert Mason

The first exhibition of Robert Mason's *Broadgate Paintings and Drawings 1989-90* will be at the Yale Center for British Art in New Haven, Conn. from September 12-November 11, 1990.

All works are in feet and inches, height x width. They are acrylic on paper (or linen), some with charcoal and oil crayon

Published by Rosehaugh Stanhope Developments plc 1990
Designed by Tamar Burchill
Photographs of Robert Mason's work by Edward Woodman
(except *Millers Tunnel I* by D. James Dee)
Typeset by Rowland (London) Ltd
Printed in England by Balding + Mansell, 5000 copies
ISBN 1 873175 00 0

Broadgate is one of London's major property developments. Built in the City on the site of Broad Street Station and adjacent to Liverpool Street Station, it covers twenty-nine acres and provides some five million square feet of new office space at the heart of the financial centre of London.

Broadgate has been developed by Rosehaugh Stanhope Developments (a joint venture between Rosehaugh plc and Stanhope Properties plc) in partnership with the British Rail Property Board. The active support of the London Borough of Hackney and the Corporation of the City of London with regard to the arts as well as the architecture has enabled Broadgate to achieve an exciting identity and to become a new place within the City.

Works of art are an integral part of the scheme. The developers are committed to 'percent for art' whereby a fixed proportion of the development cost is spent on works of art. The sculptures include Richard Serra's imposing *Fulcrum* in the Octagon; George Segal's *Rush Hour*, Jacques Lipchitz's *Bellerophon Taming Pegasus* in front of Security Pacific House, Howard Hodgkin's 100′ mural, Jim Dine's *Venus* sculptures and Barry Flanagan's *Leaping Hare on Crescent and Bell* in the Arena. Recently works by Stephen Cox, Sol LeWitt, Michael Craig-Martin, Corbero and Fernando Botero have been installed. Craft, metalwork and ceramics play a part in creating this welcoming environment.

Robert Mason's imaginative paintings of the people who made possible the construction of Broadgate are worthy records of the endeavour that has gone into making Broadgate the success it is today.

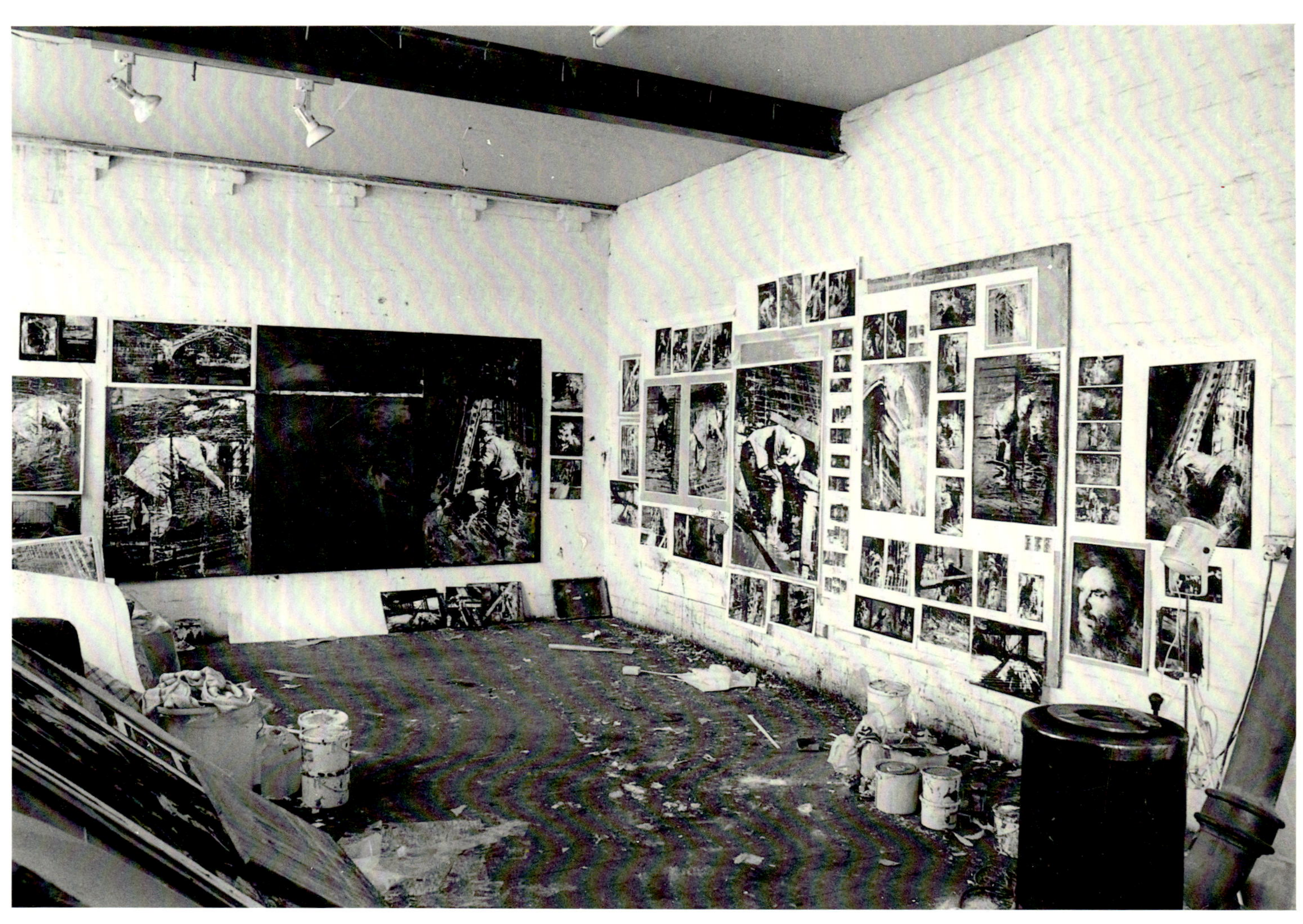

Artist's Studio, April 1989

For the last fifteen months I have had the pleasure to meet and work with an extremely dedicated group of people all of whom have been involved in the construction of Broadgate. Their enthusiasm and participation in this project allowed me to make an extended study of the site which is adjacent to Liverpool Street Station, close to my studio in Shoreditch.

I would like to thank everyone who has contributed to this commission and to name the following individuals and companies for their special involvement: Paul Lewis, Jules Allen, Fiona Revett, Julie Martin and many others at Stanhope Properties, Godfrey Bradman and his colleagues at Rosehaugh, Stan George, Dick Merrigan, Karen Patterson, Freida Davidson, Christine Jones, Ian Macpherson and Ian Wylie of the Bovis team, Harold Schiff and the others working for Schal Associates Inc, Clive Winkler and Miller Construction, Peter Foggo and Arup Associates, British Rail, Murphy's and Bruce Graham and Tom Fridstein of Skidmore, Owings and Merrill. The special commitment and active involvement of John Gosling and the unions was crucial to the commission and very much appreciated. Edward Woodman's participation in the photographic recording of the construction of Phase II and completed paintings, and his company have been of continual importance. My gratitude goes as well to Richard Burdett and Richard Cork for their response to the work and their contribution of the text for this book. I also owe thanks to Catherine Lampert, Tony Sumner, Hal Katzen, Dave White, Edna, Francis and Julia James, Danny Chau, Tamar Burchill, and Stuart Keegan. The support of Barclays Bank, Bishopsgate and Shoreditch has been much appreciated.

My deepest gratitude goes to Stuart Lipton who proposed this project and by his encouragement, patience and vision helped sustain the momentum and also allowed the work to expand into more than a year's single-minded preoccupation.

I would like to warmly thank Duncan Robinson, Director of the Yale Center for British Art who invited me to show the works in New Haven this Autumn.

This book owes everything, and is therefore dedicated, to the men and women who have planned and built Broadgate.

ROBERT MASON

BROADGATE

an urban artefact

'London is above all a metropolis of mercantilism . . .
[where] . . . the financier was an artist and the artist a financier'
JOHN SUMMERSON, *Georgian London*, 1946.

Broadgate is a product of dynamic tensions. As a development it extends the Georgian tradition of London, Summerson's 'metropolis of mercantilism . . . raised by private, not by public wealth' creating a new commercial neighbourhood on the fringes of the City. As a building project it represents a *tour de force* of engineering and construction, a 'city within a city' built in record time over and around an active railway station. As an essay in urban design it reflects the current concerns of the discipline in its search for a contemporary architectural vocabulary that respects traditional spatial rules and urban form.

In his paintings of the construction of Broadgate, Robert Mason raises similar emotions to the architecture: engagement and artifice, collectivity and individuality, vision and reality. Photographic image and painted surface are collaged and become indistinct. Architecture has always proven fertile ground for artists, from Piranesi's romantic reconstructions of Ancient Rome, the dark and brooding character of his *Carceri*, to the Futurists' fascination with the dynamic force of modern building form. Over and above questions of artistic technique, these paintings emphasise the cultural and emotional significance of architecture. They remind us of the sheer force of building form, not as a backdrop to the 'theatre of society' but as a key player in the structure of everyday life. Mason's depictions of everyday life of Broadgate, a patient narrative on the life of an architectural project, reflect the anxieties and ambiguities of this condition.

A similar neurosis prevails in architecture today. The tenets of the Modern Movement – the so-called international style – have been questioned in favour of a more critical, regional architecture that acknowledges its cultural and physical context. The built reality of the modern vision – particularly in Britain – has undergone severe scrutiny. A profound critique has emerged that proposes a critical continuation of modernism without resorting to historicist pastiche and cynical eclecticism, Broadgate, as an urban artifact, is a sign of its times. The sequence of buildings and spaces is itself a 'collage' that seeks to establish a sense of place in the City. Its public spaces are designed as forms of 'collective consciousness', places where people gather, which carry the imprint of urban life. The designs by Arup Associates and Skidmore, Owings and Merrill reflect an understanding of the spatial structure of historic London yet they reveal an appreciation of the modern American city where private enterprise contributes to the quality of public realm both inside and outside buildings.

The Broadgate master plan is founded on intelligibility and integration as a conscious rejection of the labyrinthine confusion of its modernist

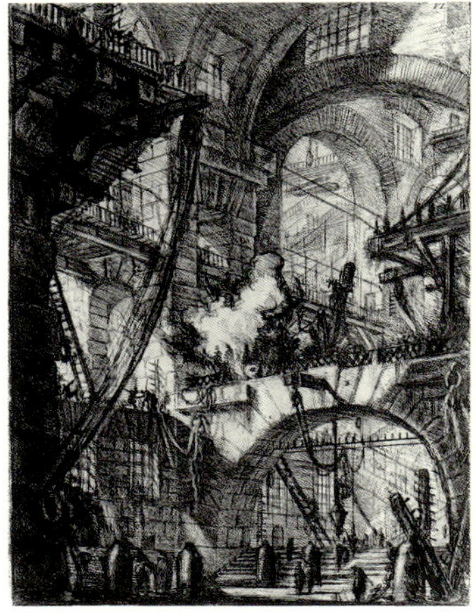

Piranesi, *Carceri*

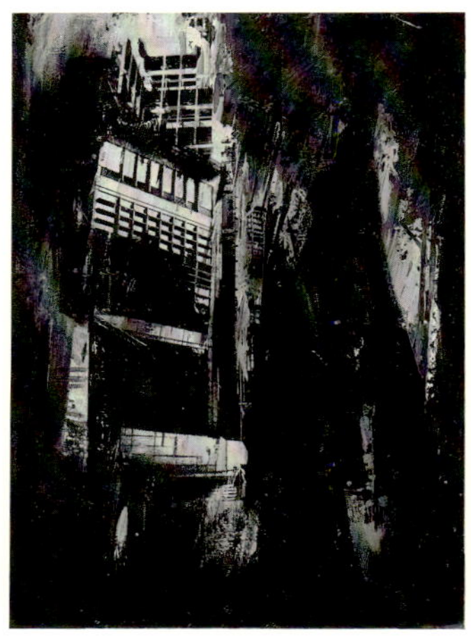

first panel *Night and Day*

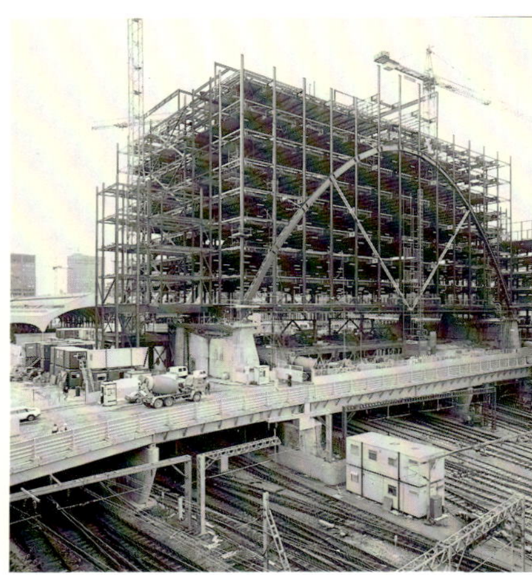

Exchange House, Phase II in construction

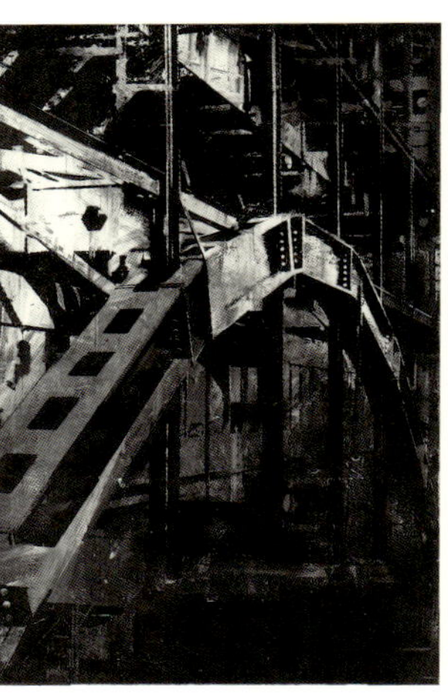

Phase II

counterparts. The new quarter is organised around as series of public spaces with distinct geometric forms: a square, a circle and rectangle. Each space is linked by pedestrian alleys and paths that extend and complement the existing pattern of streets in the neighbouring areas. It is a dense network of spaces punctuated by strong architectonic and sculptural forms.

The grand arches of Exchange House, a distinctive landmark in London's skyline, are a pure expression of the structural essence of the building which spans the railway tracks into Liverpool Street Station. The building is both suspended and supported by the parabolic arches giving rise to a spacious public plaza below. Its steel structure is fully exposed as a result of the development of innovative fire-resisting technology, a veritable engineering feat reminiscent of visual force of Victorian railway structures.

The buildings surrounding Broadgate Circle establish a dialogue between the solidity of the granite and the transparency of steel and glass. The luminous atrium spaces and the glass and steel domes establish a clear architectural framework which unifies the character of the public open spaces. There is an interplay of the different geometries of building forms that create a varied and complex urban landscape.

The range of architectural expression in the buildings of Broadgate, the richness of materials – from granite and steel, to terracotta and glass – the variety of formal compositions and the exploration of new spatial languages are symptomatic of their times: an architecture of consensus where variety is preferred to homogeneity, where individual expression predominates over global order.

The disposition of the buildings and their detailed design seem to emphasise movement, the very movement of people thronging to and from Liverpool Street Station on a daily basis. The facades are screens for the interior – the 'shell and core' modern office building – yet they respond and give shape to the architecture of the exterior. While there is variety of architectural vocabulary from building to building, each is designed with a

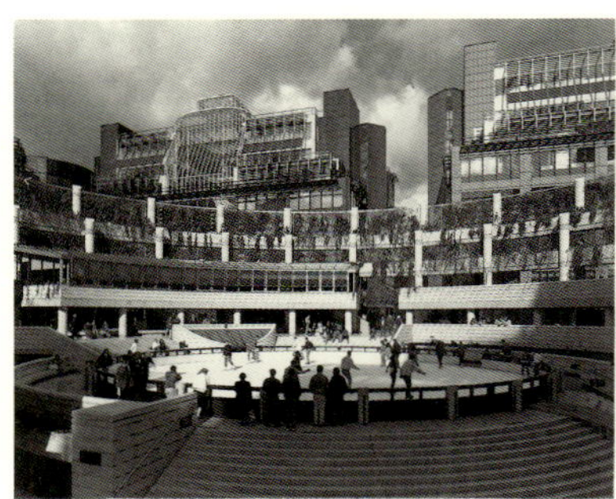

Broadgate ice rink

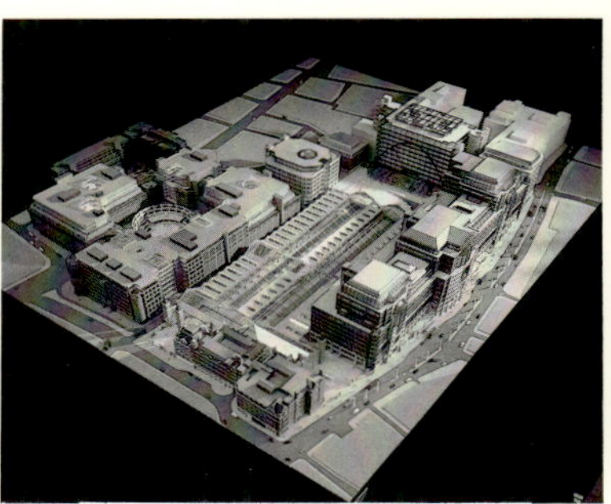

Broadgate, view of model

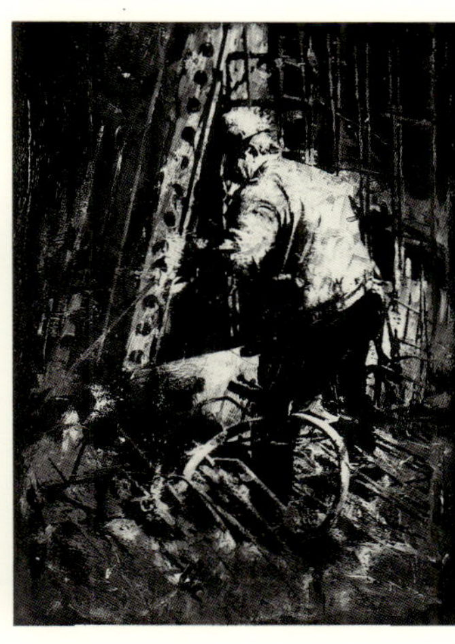

right panel *Workers Broadgate*

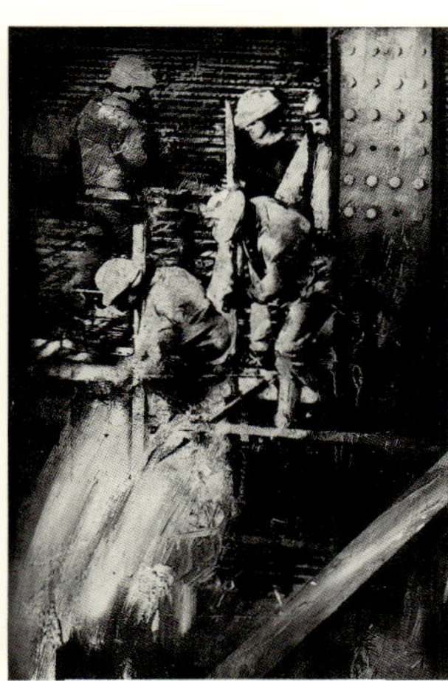

Phase II Rainy Day

degree of internal consistency and rigour. The buildings are not objects floating in space but maintain continuity of the street edge. Thus, the sense of containment, the relation between an individual and his environment is kept constant. The eye is nonetheless distracted with changing materials and textures, unexpected vistas and visual alignments.

The colours, shapes and patterns of the architecture are reflected in Mason's paintings. They expose the very essence of Broadgate – quite literally, they reveal how it is made, where the joints are, what it feels like. The paintings accentuate the force and presence of the structures. They do not attempt to *represent* a reality. They *constitute* a reality on the canvas. Mason as an artist depicts the deeper qualities of the architecture without resorting to superficial respresentations (commonly employed by architects) which mystify and neutralise the architectural object. His paintings strive to depict the architecture as an urban artefact transcending the photographic and the documentary.

Broadgate has now achieved a critical mass. Yet it is in a state of flux. New buildings and spaces have just been completed. Other buildings are being designed and discussed. The surroundings, which in part have given shape and meaning to the project, are themselves changing. Mason's paintings provide a narrative, a document of its growth, its 'rites of passage' from adolescence to maturity. Once complete, Broadgate will suffer a loss. It will lose the intrinsic vitality of its construction – the sweat, the activity and the continuous occupation so vividly depicted by Mason. The intensity of production will be replaced by the comfort of completion. Its spaces will become empty as the last commuters leave Exchange Square. The noise, movement and dynamism of the construction site will give way to, perhaps, a lonely silence for those who have inhabited Mason's paintings.

RICHARD BURDETT

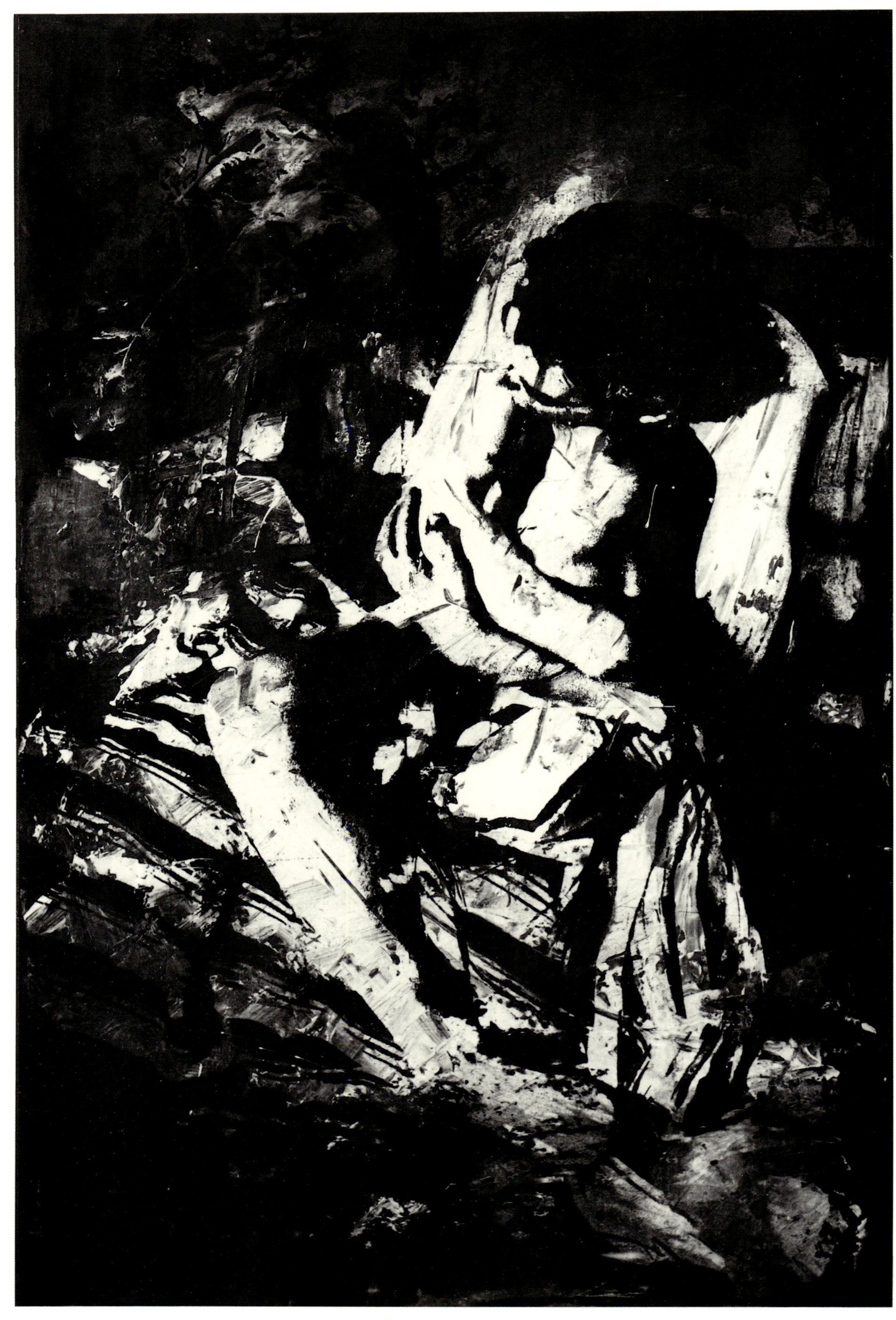

Stalking a Lost Deed 1987

Before Robert Mason became immersed in the Broadgate paintings, he might well have seemed the least likely artist to tackle such a subject. For many years his work was haunted by *memento mori* – animal carcasses and human skulls which testified to his preoccupation with private tragedy. Mason's parents, brother and sister all died when he was a child, and this multiple trauma understandably dominated his work. He became as obsessed by loss and grief as the male figure who appeared in a number of his paintings around the mid-1980s. Whether slumped or crouching, this hunched man seemed marooned in a shadowy region which intensified his sense of bereavement and isolation. Only the flaring predominance of red, ochre and warm yellow gave Mason's brooding pictures a resilience which suggested he would one day emerge from the otherwise pervasive gloom.

With hindsight, we can see how the personification of the artist in these elegiac images seems to be waiting for a means of escape from introspection. The opportunity finally arrived in January 1989, when Stuart Lipton invited him to consider painting a picture based on the activity at Broadgate for his new office. Instead of continuing to burrow into his boyhood distress, Mason found himself confronted with the challenge of looking outwards. Meditative dejection in the shadows of a claustrophobic room was now replaced by scenes of epic endeavour on one of London's most ambitious development sites. The shift of focus could hardly be more extreme, and Mason might easily have felt daunted by the unaccustomed demands it made.

In the event, however, Lipton's suggestion proved as productive, in its way, as Kenneth Clark's proposal in 1940 that Stanley Spencer travel to Lithgow's Shipyard at Port Glasgow. As chairman of the newly-formed War Artists' Advisory Committee, Clark asked Spencer to produce a painting of the strenuous shipbuilding initiative on Clydeside. Clark must have appreciated that he was asking a great deal of a visionary artist who, obsessed by life in his native Cookham, rarely strayed far beyond the village's boundaries. But Spencer accepted the challenge with a boyish eagerness which belied his true age. Having journeyed to Port Glasgow and discovered at the shipyard a sense of community just as strong as the one he cherished at Cookham, the indefatigable painter embarked on a long, arduous venture which ended, six years later, with an ensemble of scroll-like canvases amounting to 154 feet in width. The final painting, an upright image intended for the centre of the ensemble, completed what Spencer clearly regarded as a secular altarpiece celebrating the flair, dedication and humane solidarity of the Lithgow's workforce.

Although *Shipbuilding on the Clyde* is in many respects very different

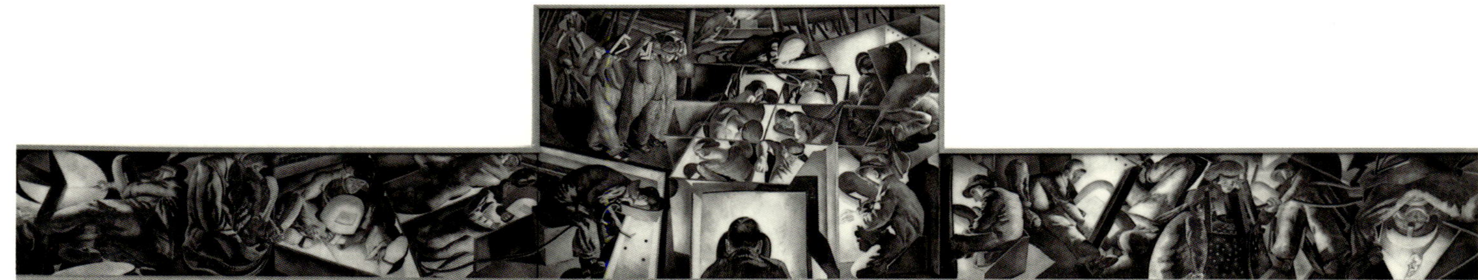

Stanley Spencer, *Shipbuilding on the Clyde*

from Mason's Broadgate sequence, the two bodies of work share a wholehearted readiness to become involved with the lives of the labouring men. Far from viewing the site at a cautious distance, and maintaining at all times a sense of fastidious detachment, Mason threw himself as eagerly as Spencer into the incessant activity he found there. Another artist might have produced a neutral account of the area, and refused to acknowledge the significance of the people responsible for constructing the buildings. Mason, however, realised at once that he wanted to concentrate on the workforce rather than the architecture. His attention was seized by the men who, largely unseen by anyone except their closest colleagues, erect these monumental developments and then move on. While the finished structure often attracts considerable attention, they normally gain no accolades for their titanic efforts from the outside world.

Despite his recent period of inward-looking work, Mason was predisposed to favour the course of action he pursued. Earlier in his career he had, after all, made a prolonged series of assemblages based on the urban dereliction opposite his East End studio. These concerns turned out to have fruitful connections with the raw activity he found at the Broadgate site, likewise visible from his studio window. Moreover, Mason had little difficulty in breaking down the instinctive suspicion with which he was regarded on his first visit. His own father was a Yorkshire lorry driver, and just before the Broadgate proposal arrived he had been planning to produce portraits of the local people he relishes drinking with in his neighbourhood pub. One of the pictures complete by January 1989 was a portrait of the man who makes regular deliveries of coal to Mason's studio building. In certain ways, therefore, he was well-prepared to cope with the immense, complex and potentially overwhelming spectacle which greeted him at Broadgate.

Like Spencer before him, Mason soon abandoned the notion of restricting himself to one painting. It was the first time he had worked with living people, and they quickly ousted his previous confessional emphasis on mortality. The presence of decay was still very apparent, in the old buildings which still required demolition before the development could be fully carried out. Within this general dilapidation, however, Mason became fascinated by the sense of urgency on an unusually speedy site unhampered by labour problems. The pace and pressure of the men working there probably affected his attitude in turn. For he produced around 150 pictures in seven months, impelled by the realisation that nothing he witnessed around him would last very long.

Attaining this degree of engagement meant exposing himself to a disconcerting amount of noise, dirt and potential danger. Even when equipped with hard hat and mufflers, Mason needed to call on all his reserves of stamina to deal with the stresses attendant on constant visits to the site. Whether going up to the cabin of the highest crane, or down on the night shift to move along the buildings' substructure, he learned how to deal with the exacting demands imposed by conditions which seasonal construction workers take for granted. The men he observed all operated in tightly organised teams, relying on a high level of implicit trust. They could only acquire such discipline after working together for a long time. He managed to establish a similar relationship with the photographer Edward Woodman, who accompanied Mason on many occasions and shot up to 300 rolls of film. These pictures proved indispensable, for the men could not be expected to stop working while an artist drew them.

As a result, Mason always ended up using photographic images as the foundation of his pictures. But he did not allow them to dominate the paintings he produced. His working method paralleled the men's efforts to wrest form and order from the muddy flux surrounding them. Deploying a boldly gestural use of sponges, fingers and hands, Mason commenced his images in a state of seeming confusion. The application of a drawing based on a projected photograph is, in its turn, scrubbed off with a large brush, leaving a monoprint-like residue in the pigment. Only at the final stage are the full resources of painting brought into play, in order to impose definition on the earlier inchoate marks. The entire procedure therefore echoes the process of building on site, except that Mason often leaves passages of his initial, broadly handled work to impart dynamism and fluidity to scenes which might otherwise look rigid or inert.

These vigorously textured areas of the picture also express the excitement he felt while exploring the complexities of the Broadgate development. He was particularly enthralled by his journeys deep into the ground. An exhibition of Henry Moore's tube shelter drawings at the British Museum had alerted him beforehand to the possibility that the subterranean visits might be especially stimulating. All the same, nothing prepared him for the revelation of descending into the Victorian tunnels at night. Many of the paintings he produced from his underground expeditions at Broadgate have an awesome quality, as if Mason felt dwarfed by the size and penumbral mystery of the new ventilation shafts and sewers connected to the old network of tunnels.

The figures discernible in this looming, shadowy region appear dwarfed by their surroundings, whereas the workers above ground assume more prominent positions within the picture-space. Mason was fascinated by the bending, twisting and stooping figures, some wielding power tools while others relied on hand digging. Absorbed in their tasks, they are the principal performers in the extended drama enacted at Broadgate. Even the most

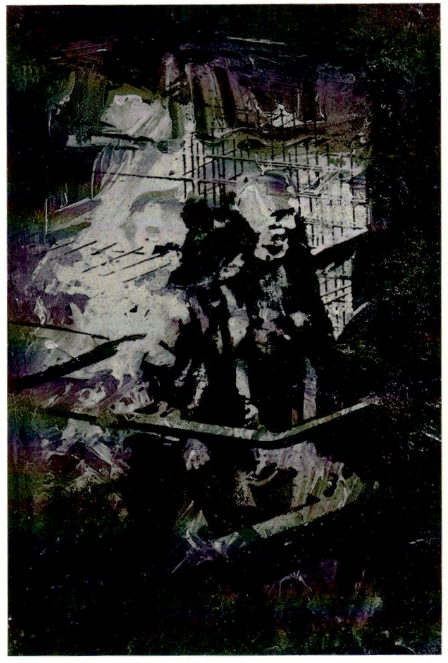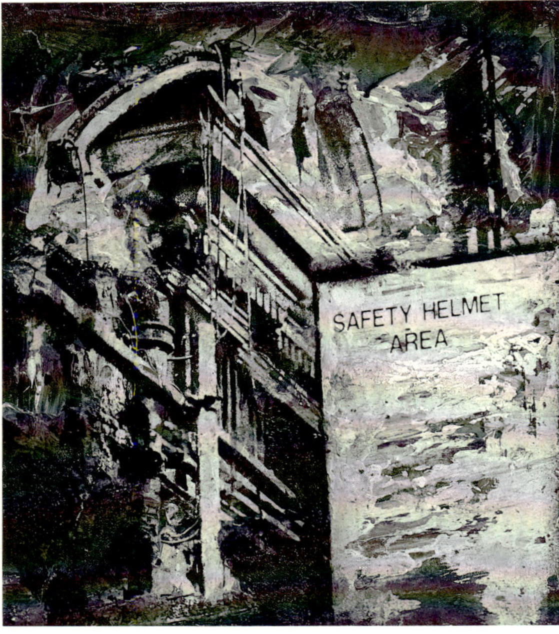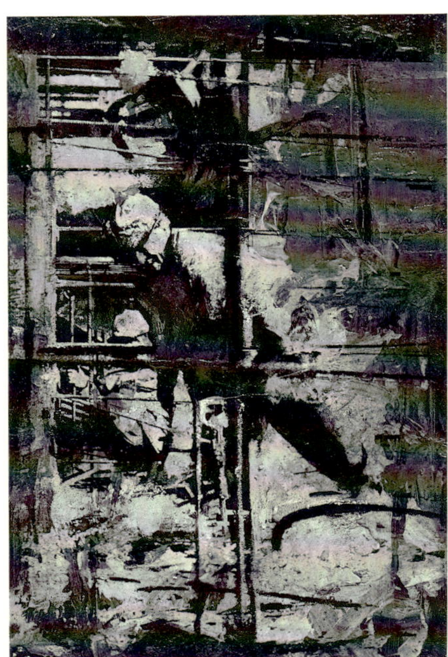

Broadgate. Three Stages 1989

manual activities have to be informed by high levels of skill and intelligence. Mason became aware of men who pause, ponder and calculate their next moves. In one triptych, the side panels of labouring figures flank a large central image dominated by a man deliberating, hand raised to chin while he decides how best to manipulate the girder resting temporarily in front of him.

Such an image reflects the exacting amount of care involved in the development of the Liverpool Street Station area in particular. At no time did the station fail to operate its services to the traveller, and in another triptych Mason incorporates a painting of commuters hurrying through the mêlée around their platform. This side panel is juxtaposed with another flanking image of workers suspended on scaffolding, but the central picture is devoted this time to an unpopulated image of a decrepit structure awaiting demolition. Its crumbling facade is invaded by a large placard warning everyone about the dangers of neglecting to wear a safety helmet in the vicinity. The painting sums up Mason's instinctive awareness of the dissolution to be found at Broadgate, and his recognition that construction on such a major inner-city site entails an enormous amount of devastation before the new architecture can arise.

On the whole, Mason avoided depicting the completed structures, preferring instead to emphasize the turmoil and strain which always lies behind the deceptively calm facade of a finished building. But in one four-panel work (see page 45), he alternates images of labouring figures with paintings of the environment they are creating. Commissioned sculpture plays an important role at Broadgate, and one of these panels contrasts the lean, rusted severity of Richard Serra's soaring *Fulcrum* with the massive elaboration of the Arup Associates building nearby. The other panel, however, concentrates on the most Serra-like aspect of the architecture: the muscularity of the Skidmore, Owings and Merrill building which spans the railway tracks with spectacular *élan*. Mason chose to depict it under construction, so that he could savour the tautness of the exposed steel units as they leap through space in a sturdy yet acrobatic arc.

Ultimately, though, people remain the dominant theme in these paintings. Mason's profound respect for the construction workers runs through the entire sequence and gives it a unifying coherence. Grave and intent, their figures attain at times an unselfconscious dignity which honours the true extent of their achievement. In one picture, a group of men are shown putting out plastic sheeting to protect welding work from the rain. As they stoop and kneel on the vertiginous perch, their bodies form themselves into an ensemble reminiscent of a Deposition group. Spencer, who gave his great Clydeside cycle a sacramental dimension, would have understood why Mason was able to invest this workaday incident with an unforced yet elevated significance.

RICHARD CORK

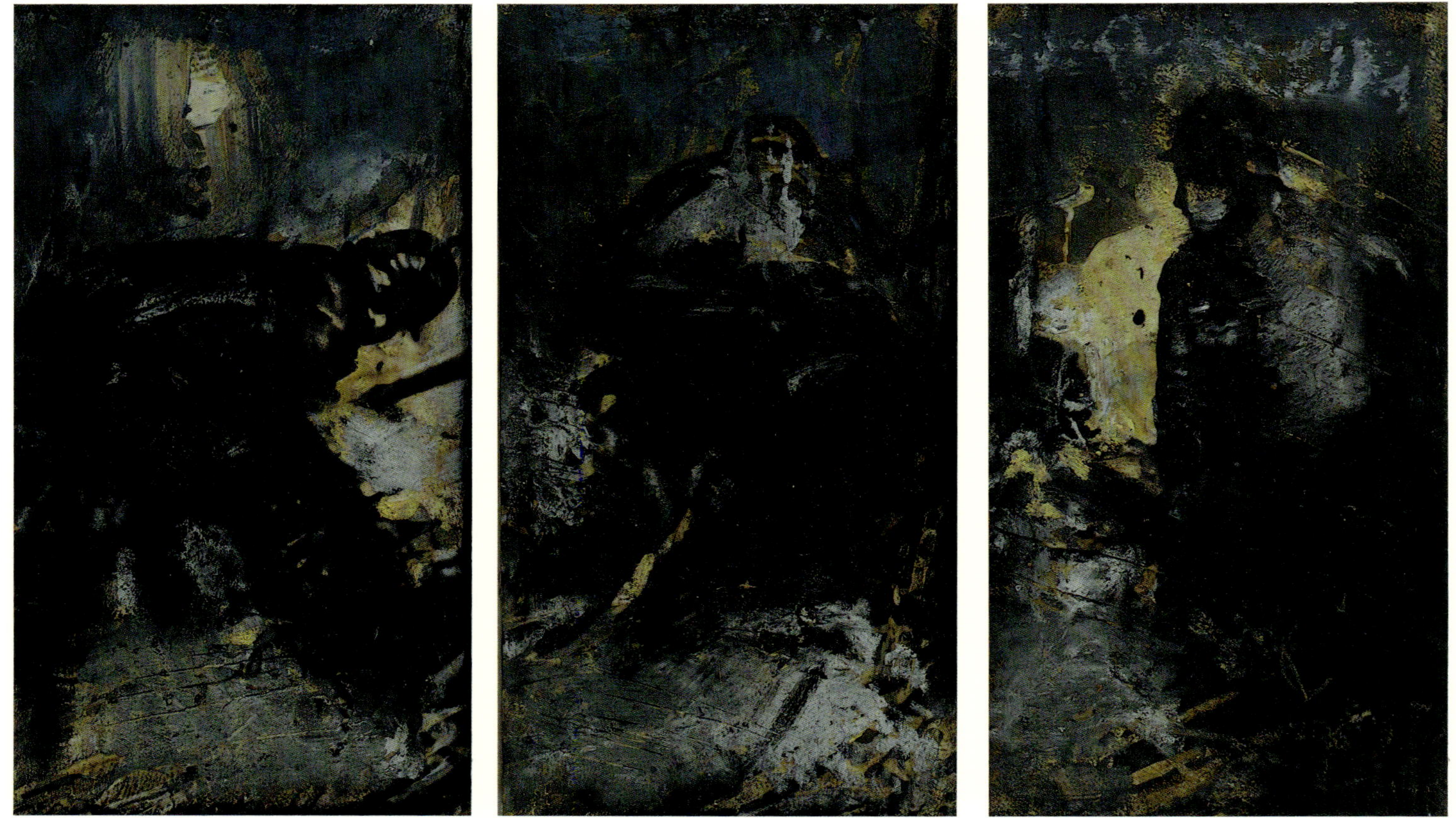

THREE STUDIES FROM THE FIRST NIGHTSHIFT 1989

16

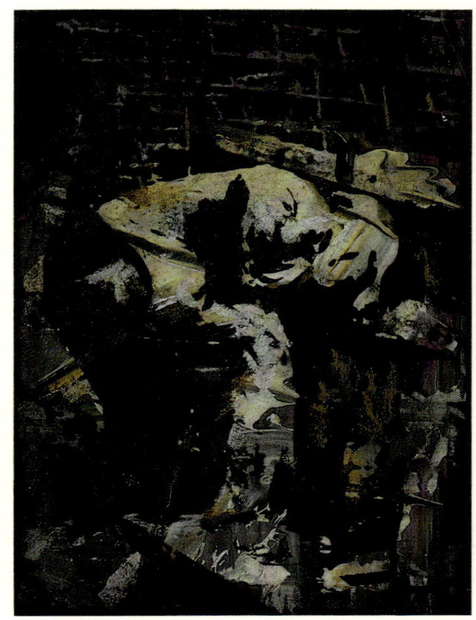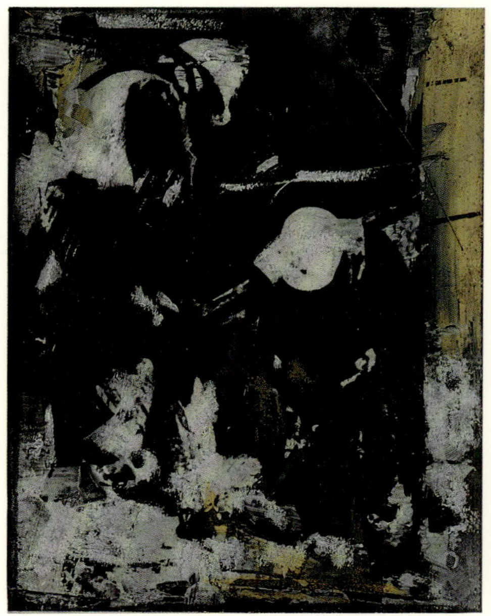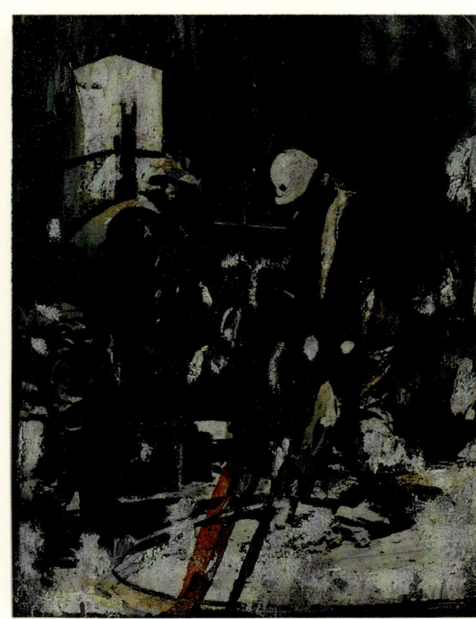

THREE STUDIES FROM BROADGATE 1989

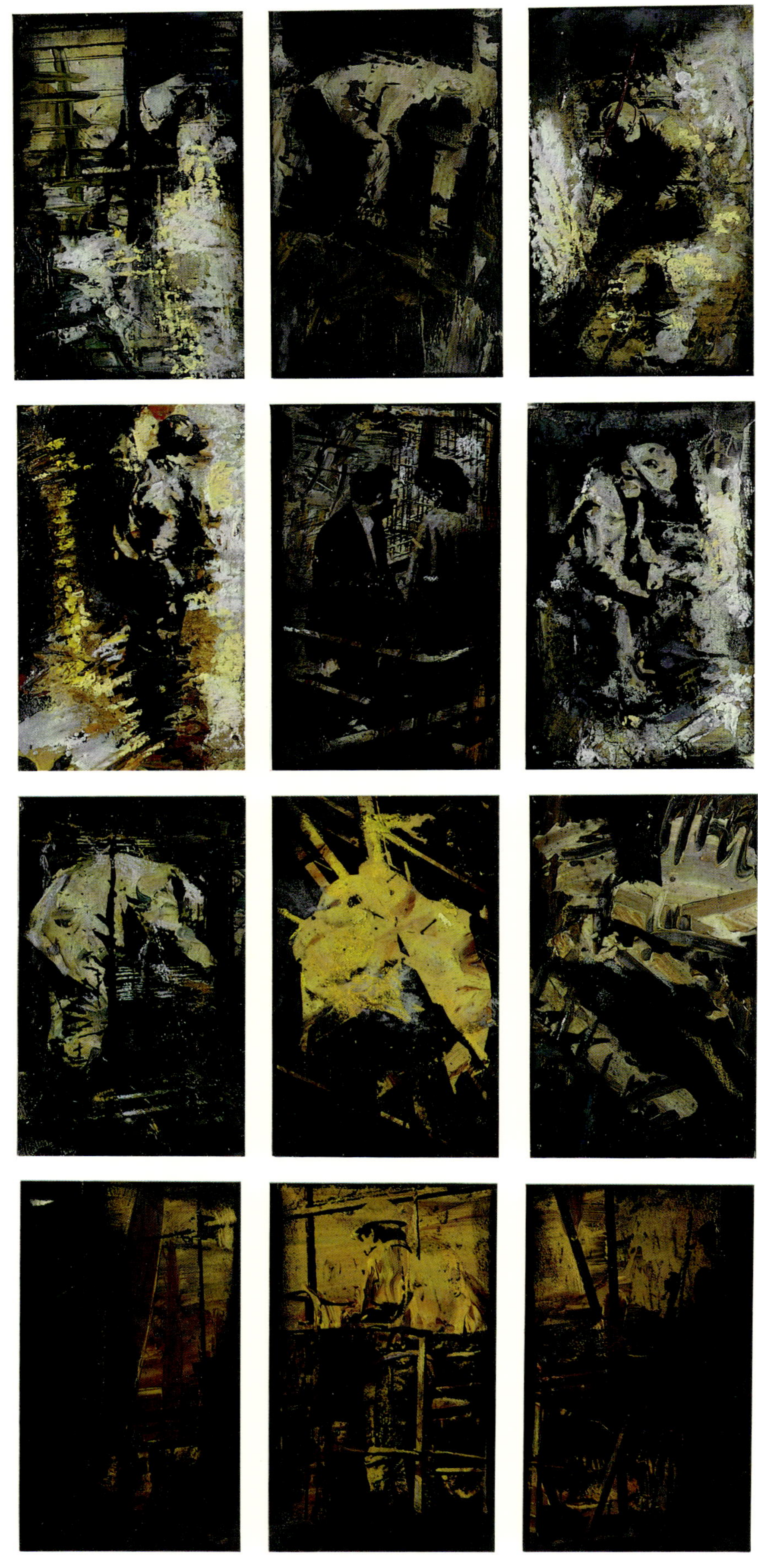

SKETCHBOOK STUDIES MARCH 1989

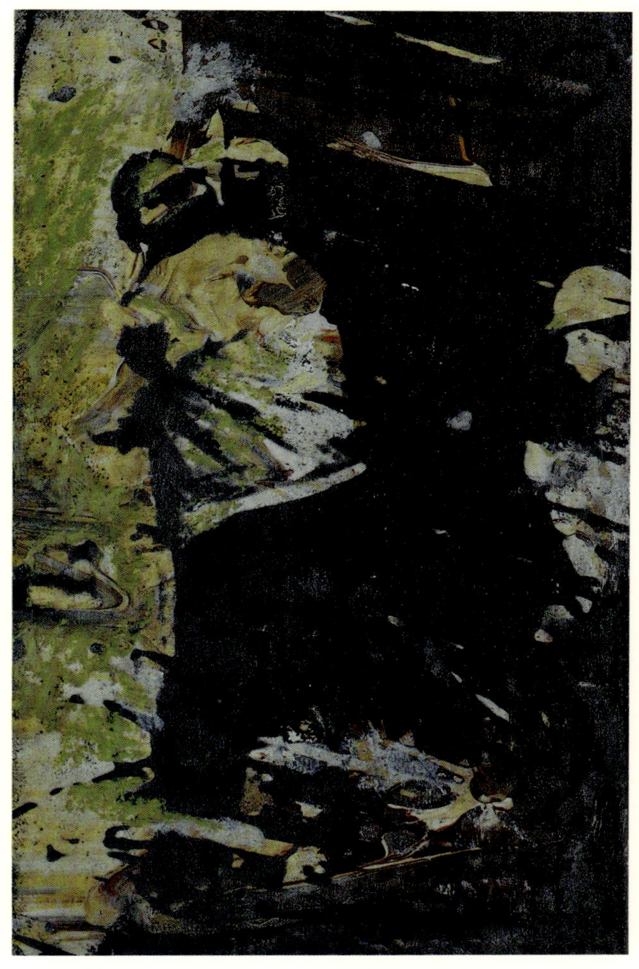 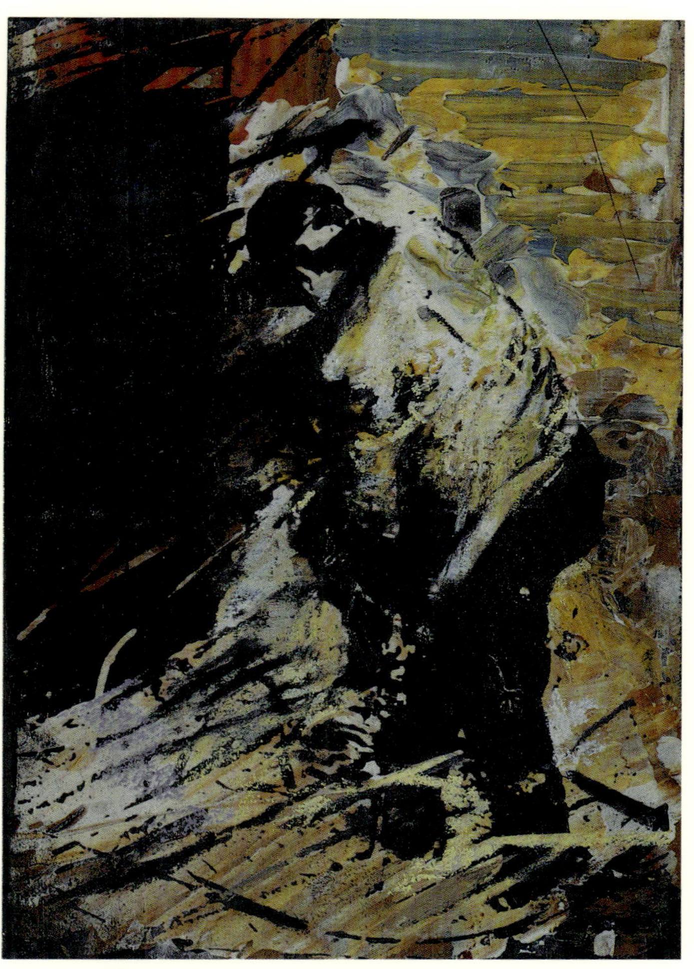

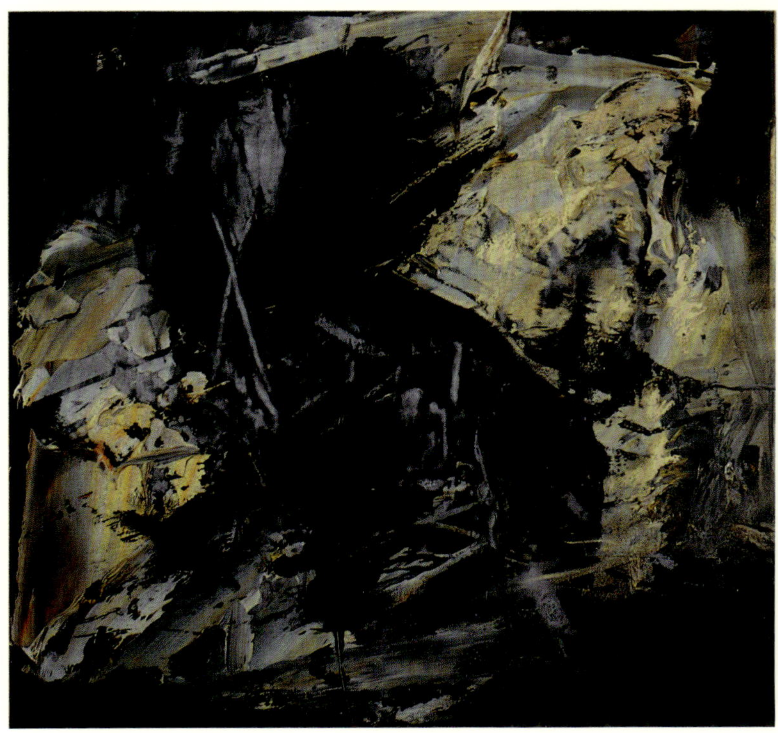 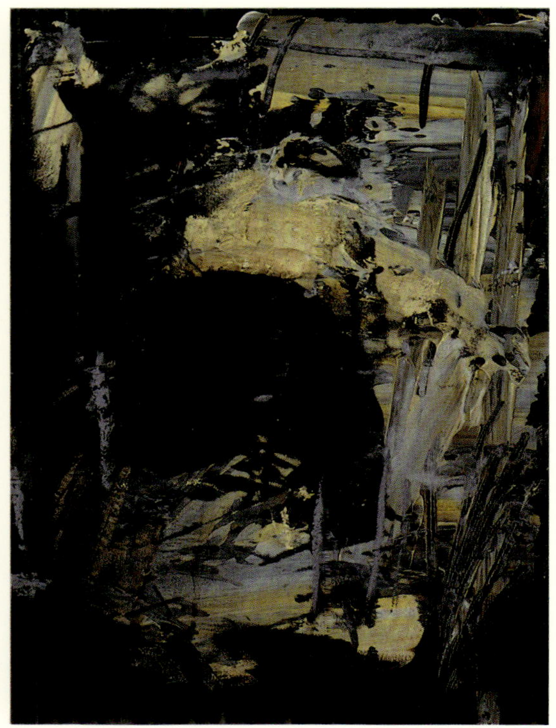

TWO STUDIES FROM THE NIGHTSHIFT 1989
TWO STUDIES FROM THE NIGHTSHIFT 1989

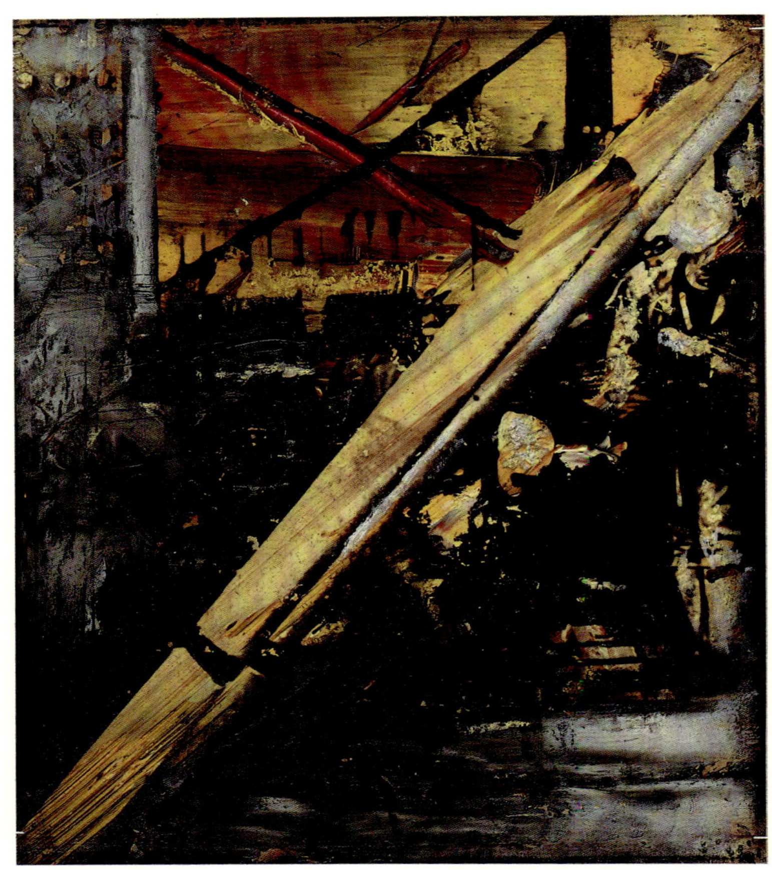 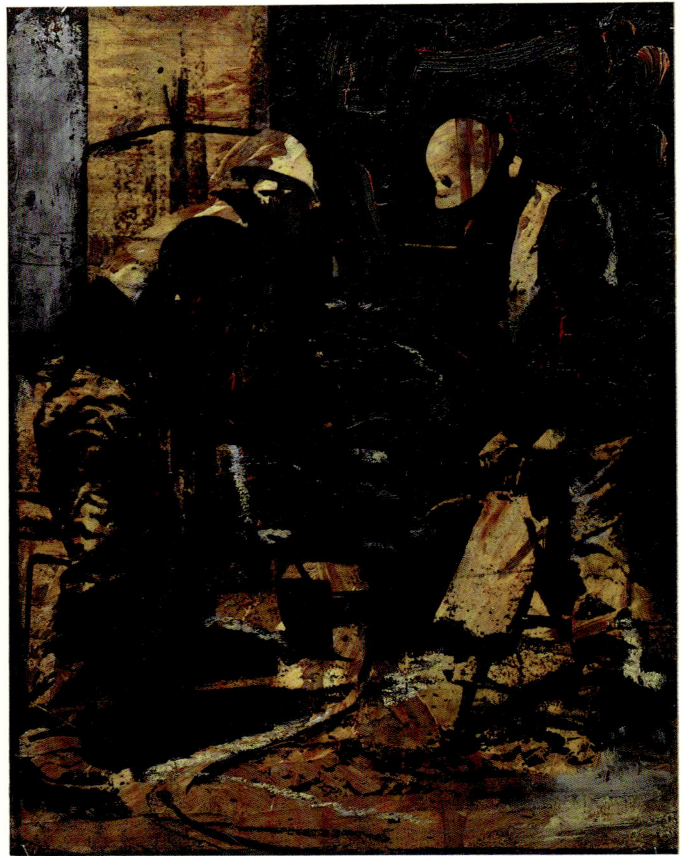

TWO STUDIES, PHASE II 1989

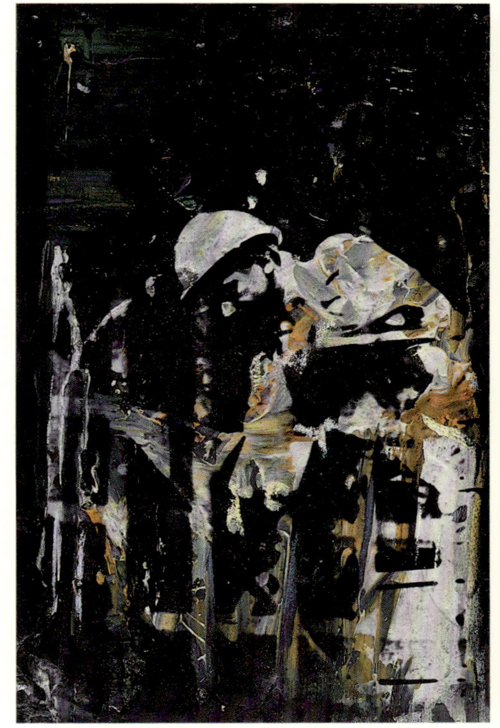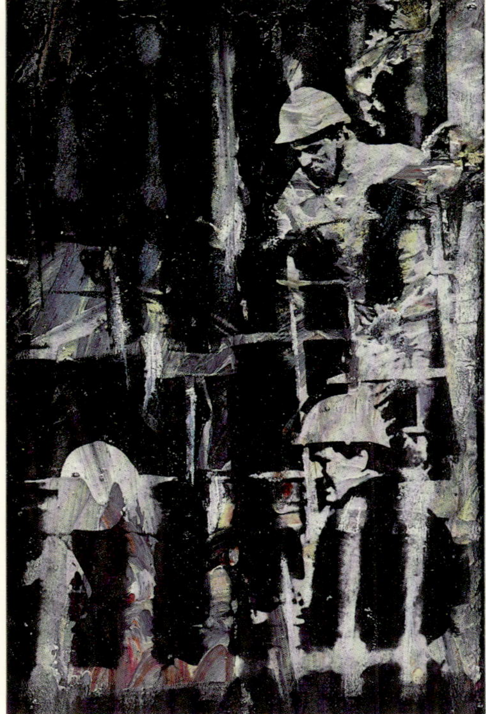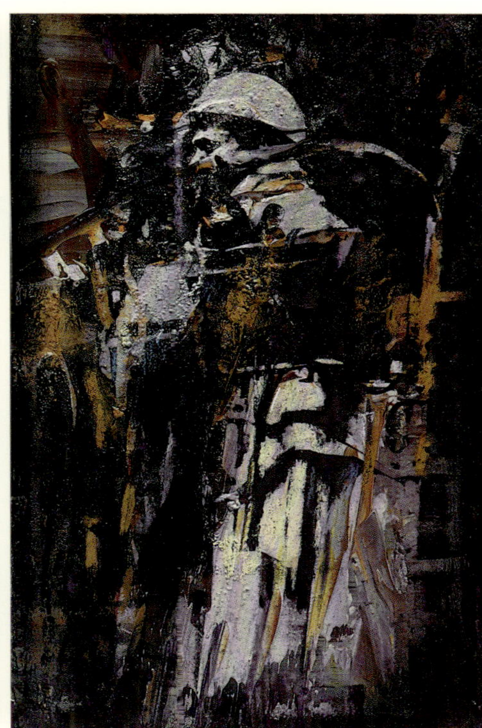

WORKING ON PHASES 6-8 BISHOPSGATE 1989

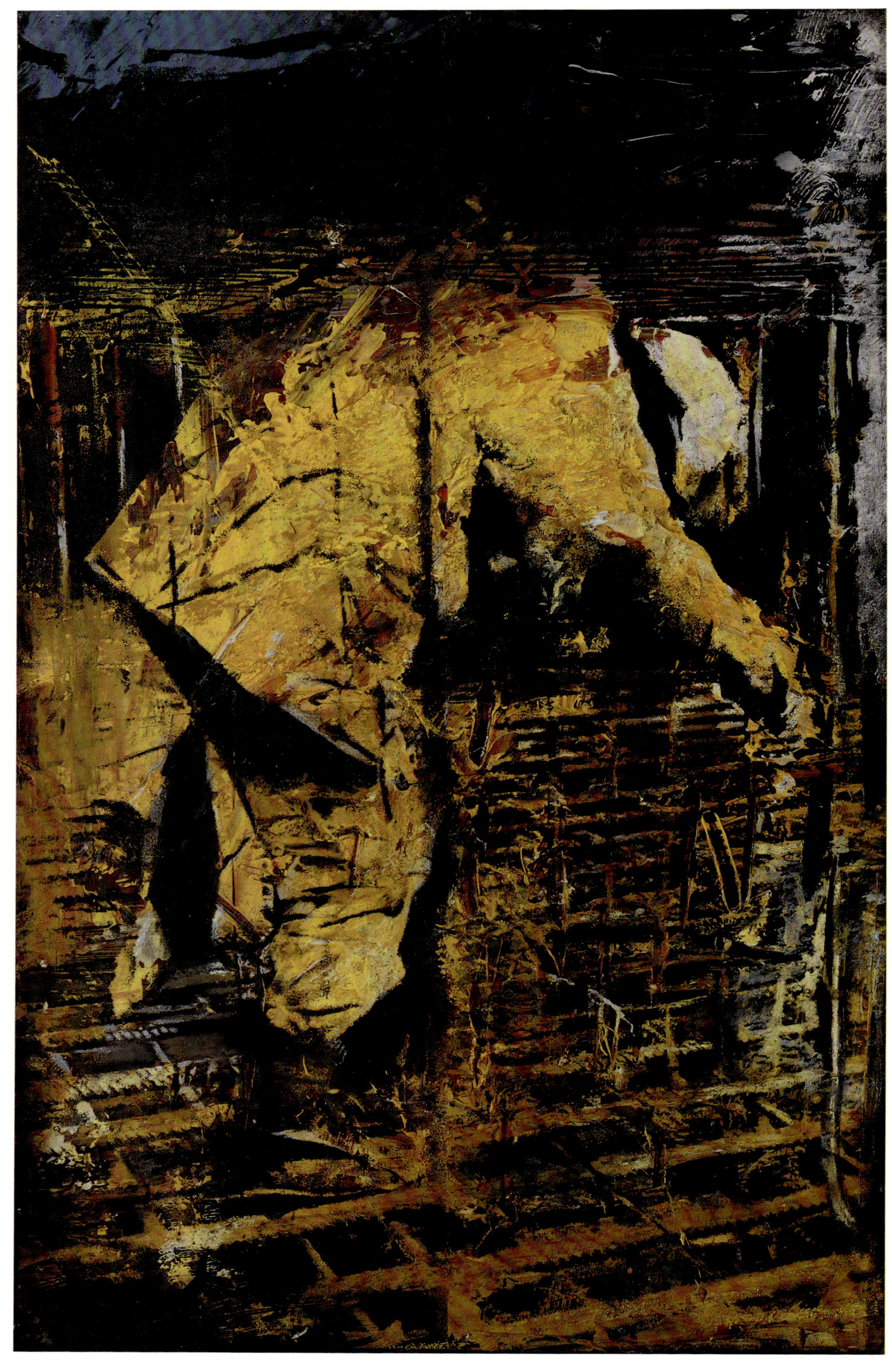

STOOPING FIGURE 1989

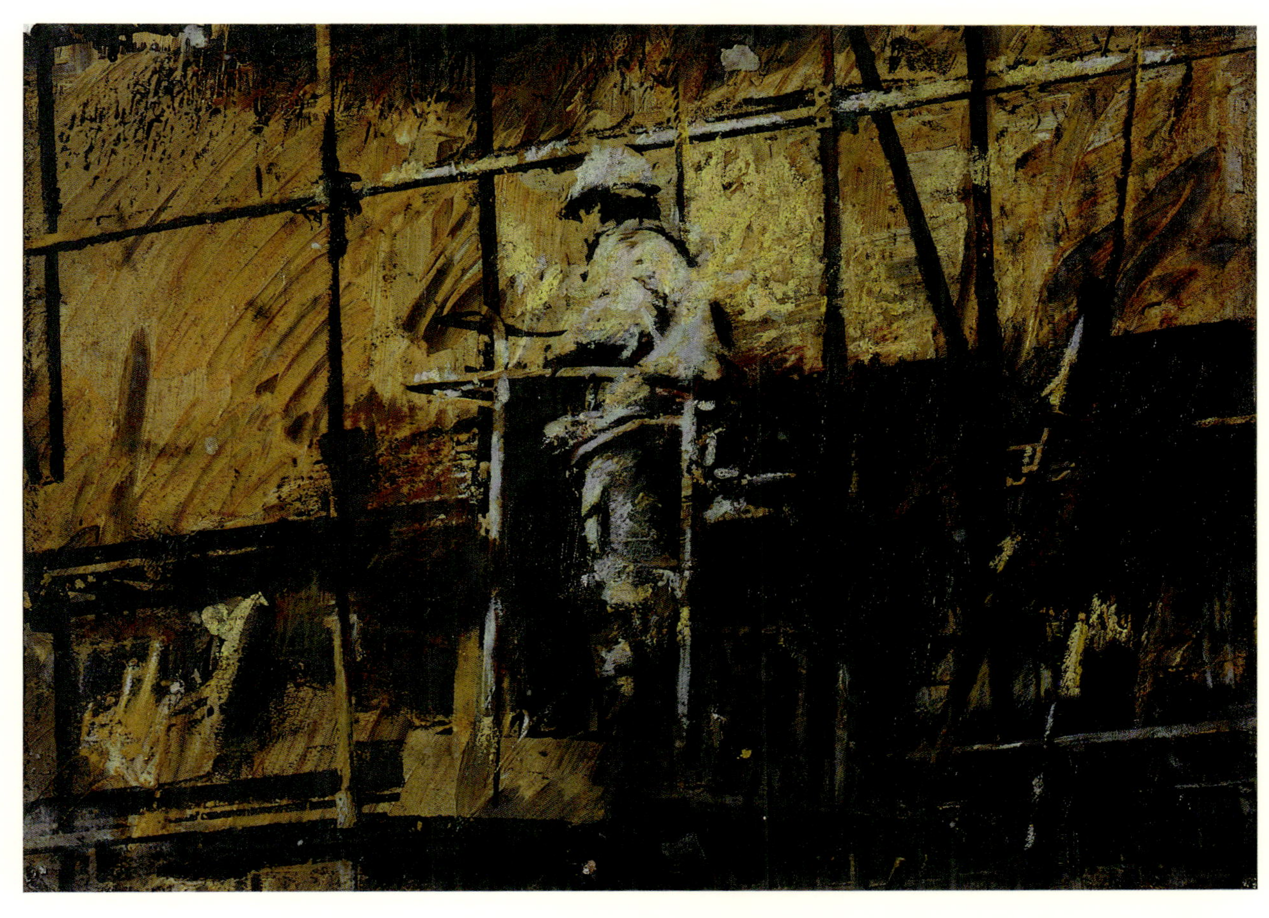

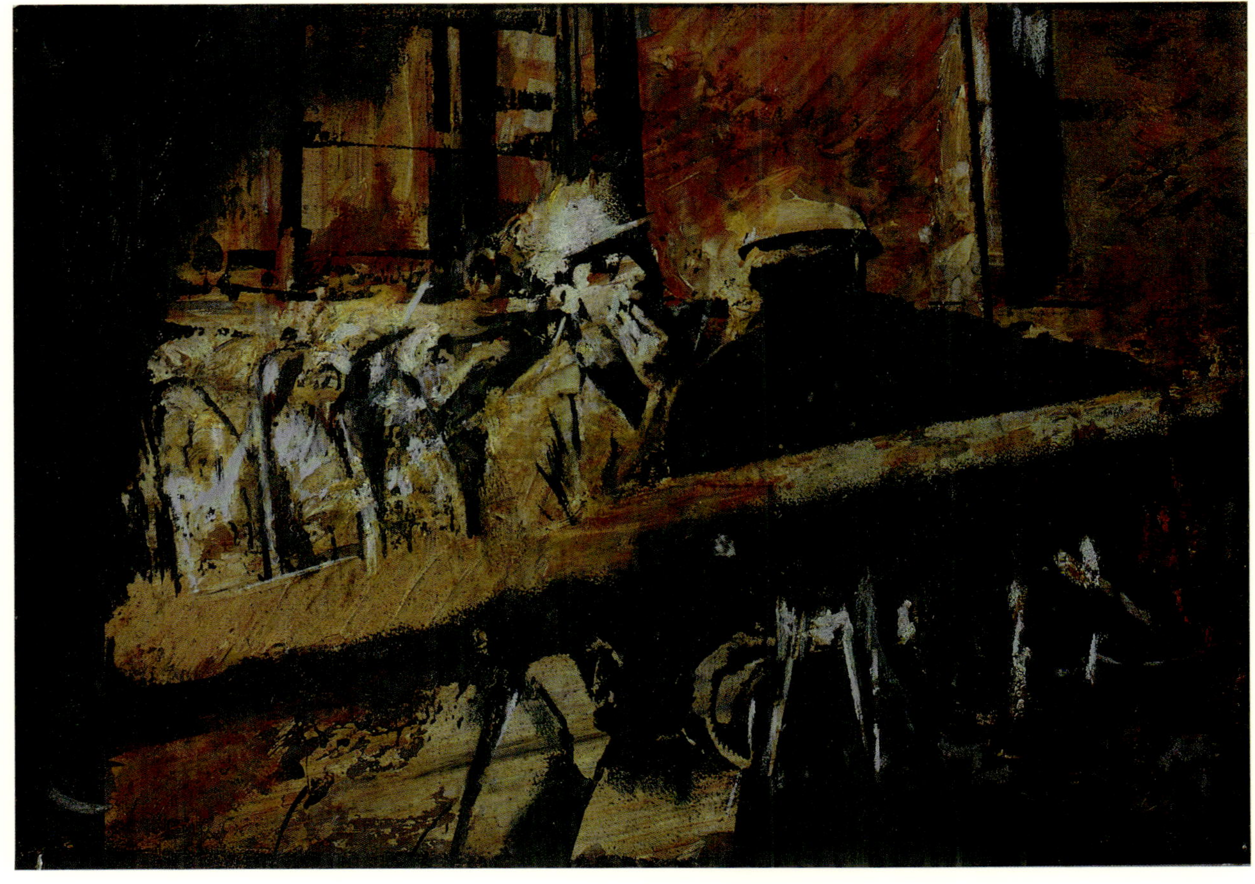

WORKING ON PHASE 6 1989

STUDY FOR THINKER 1989

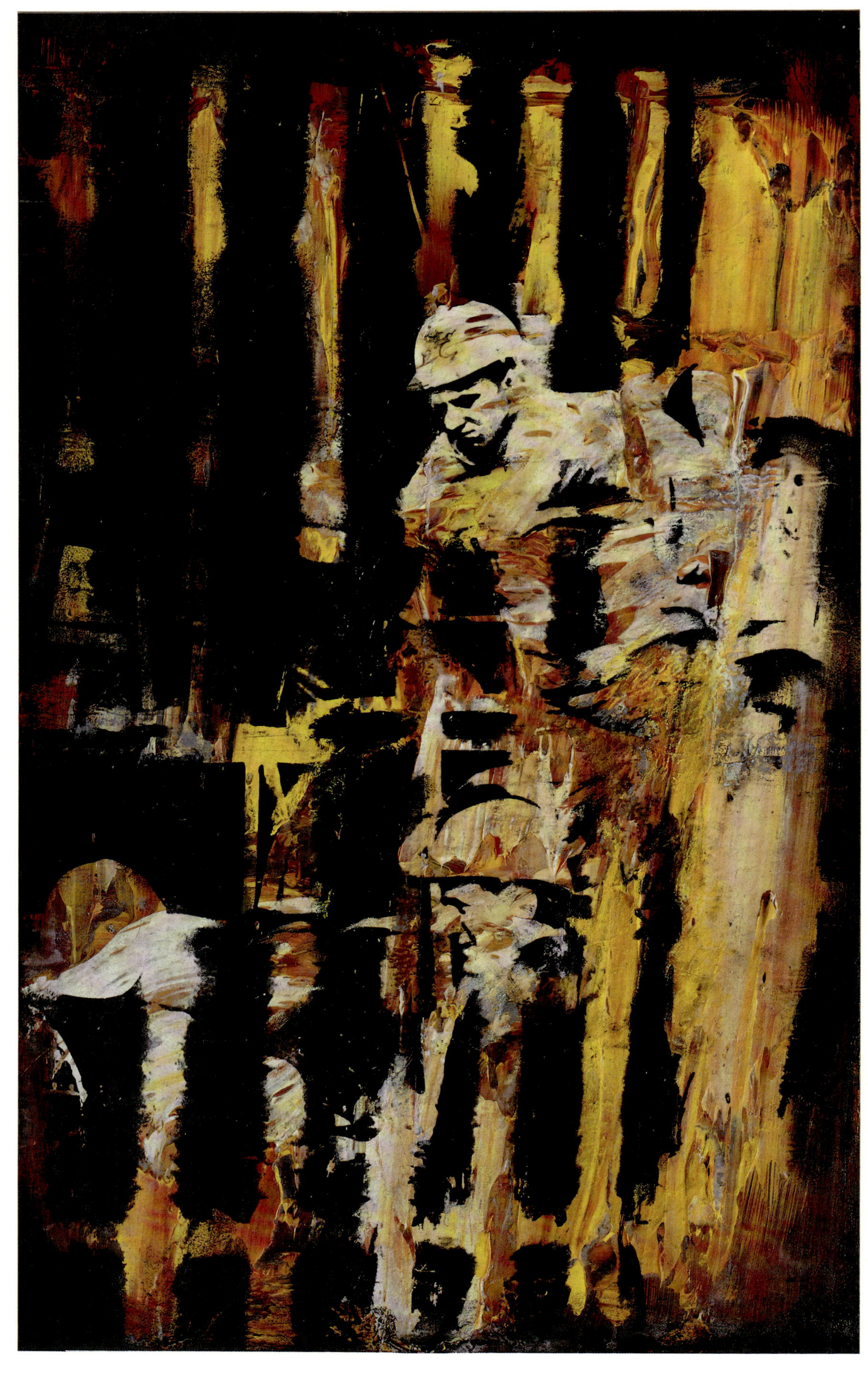

WORKING ON PHASE 6 BROADGATE 1989

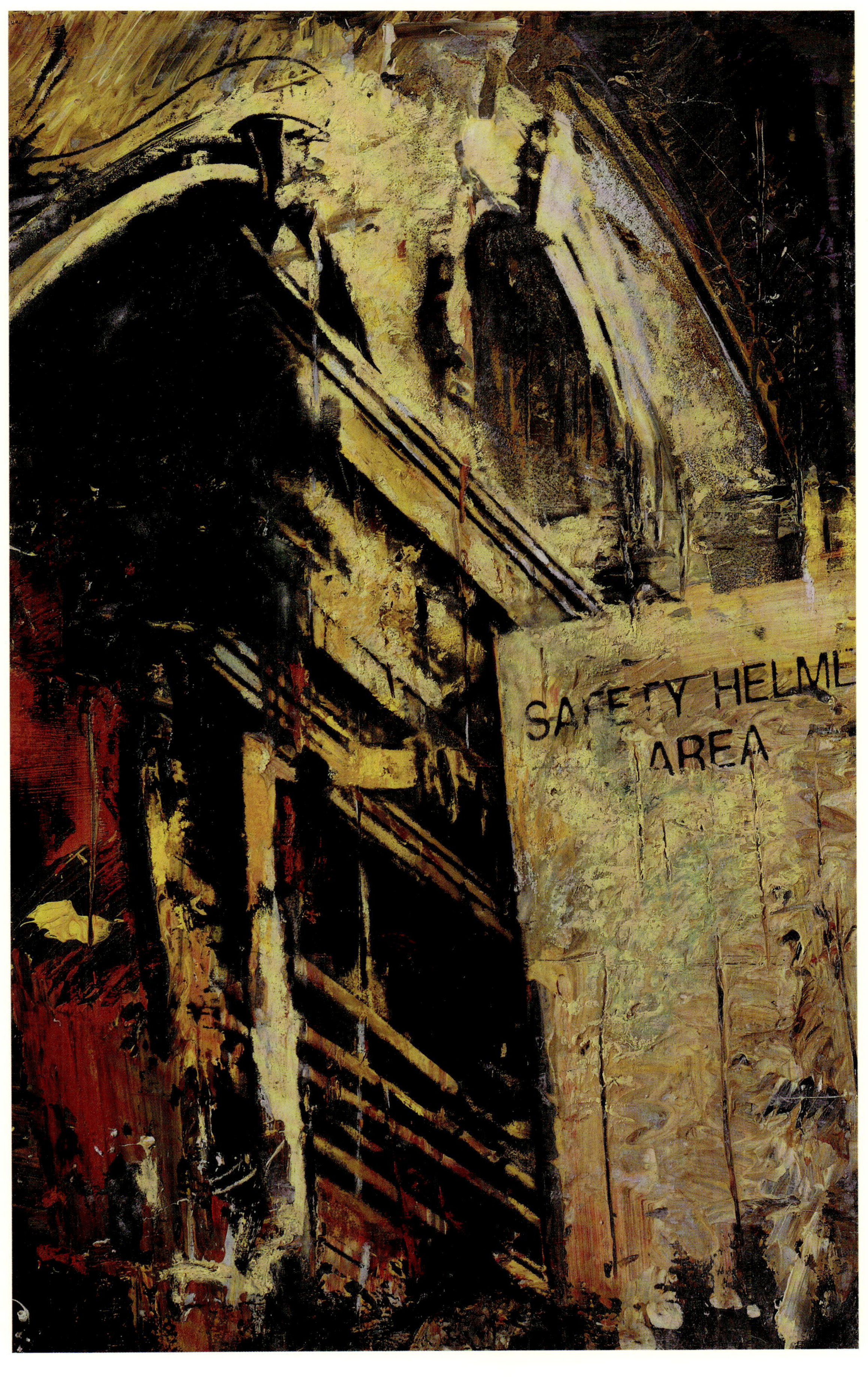

SAFETY HELMET AREA 1989

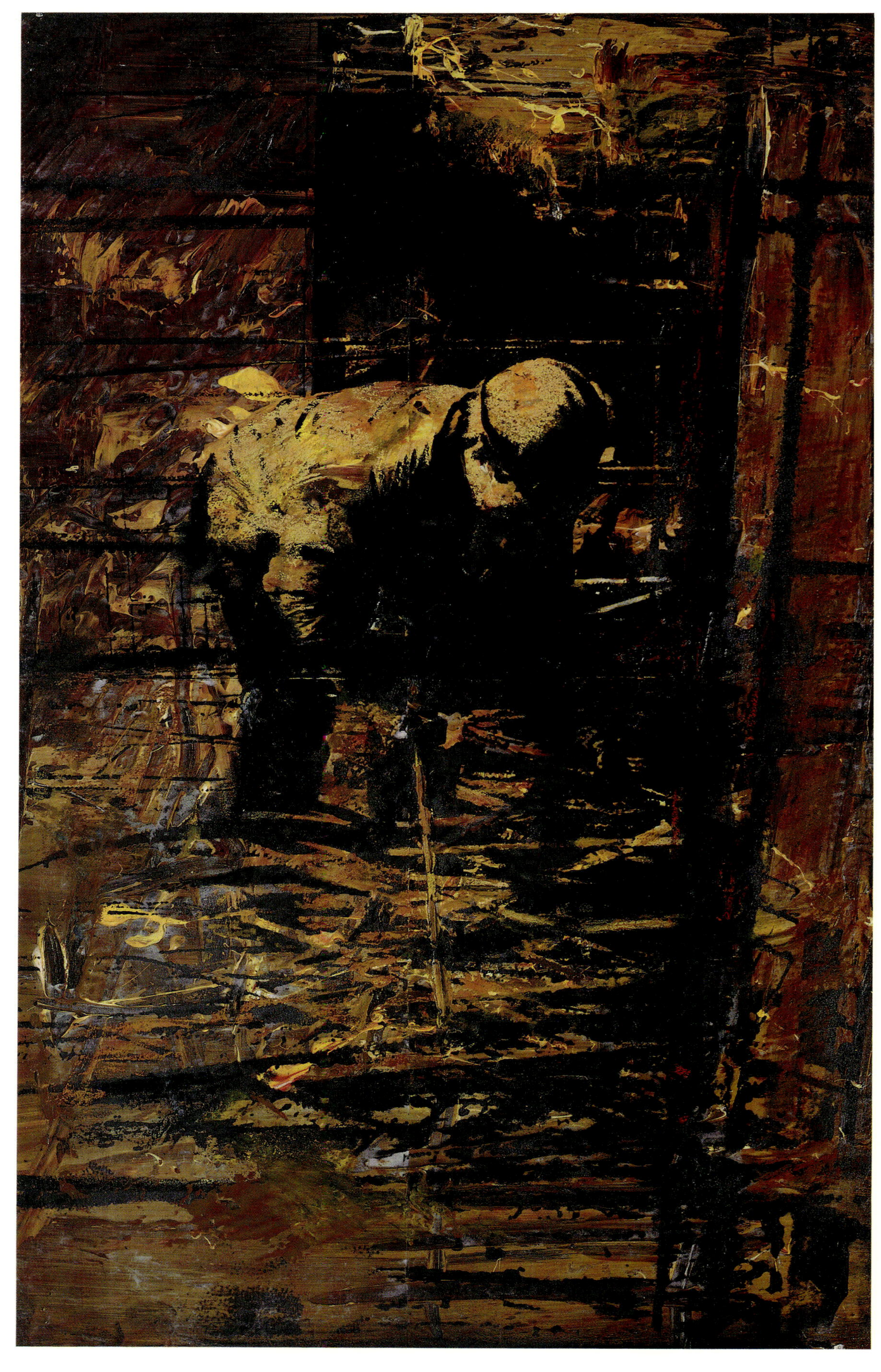

BENDING FIGURE. PLATFORM WORK 1989

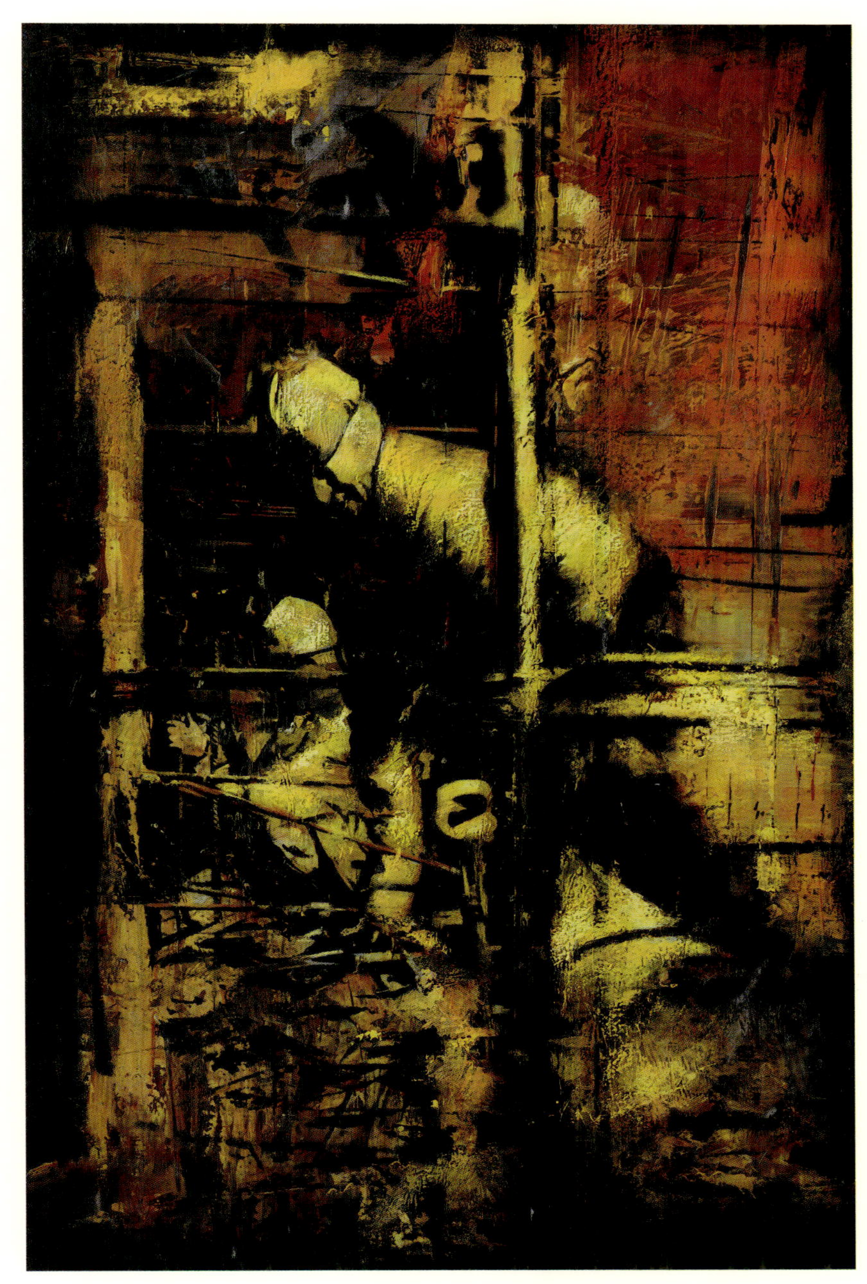

WORKERS, NIGHTSHIFT 1989-90

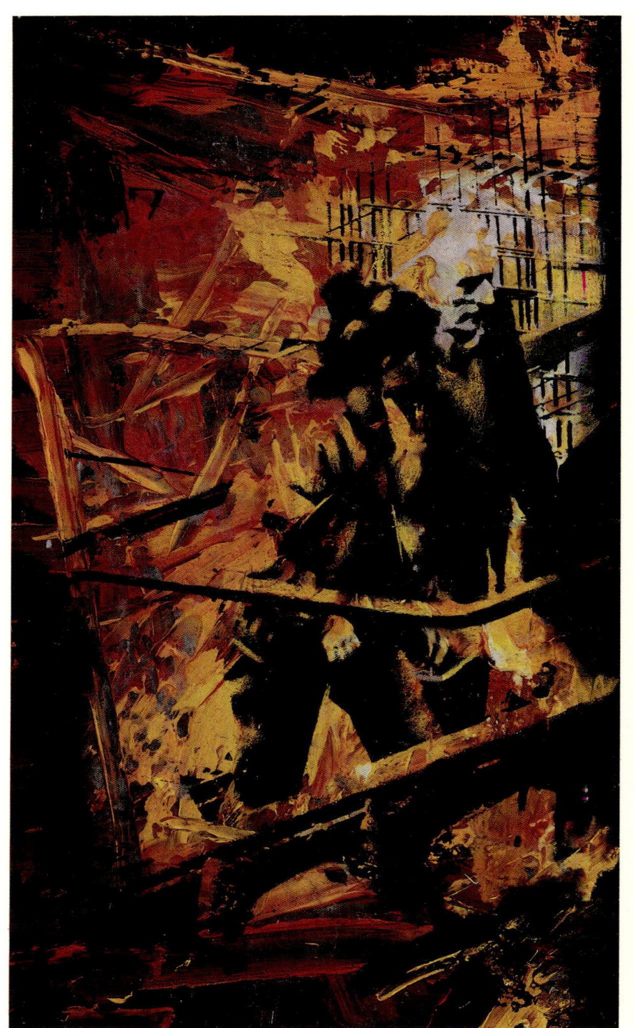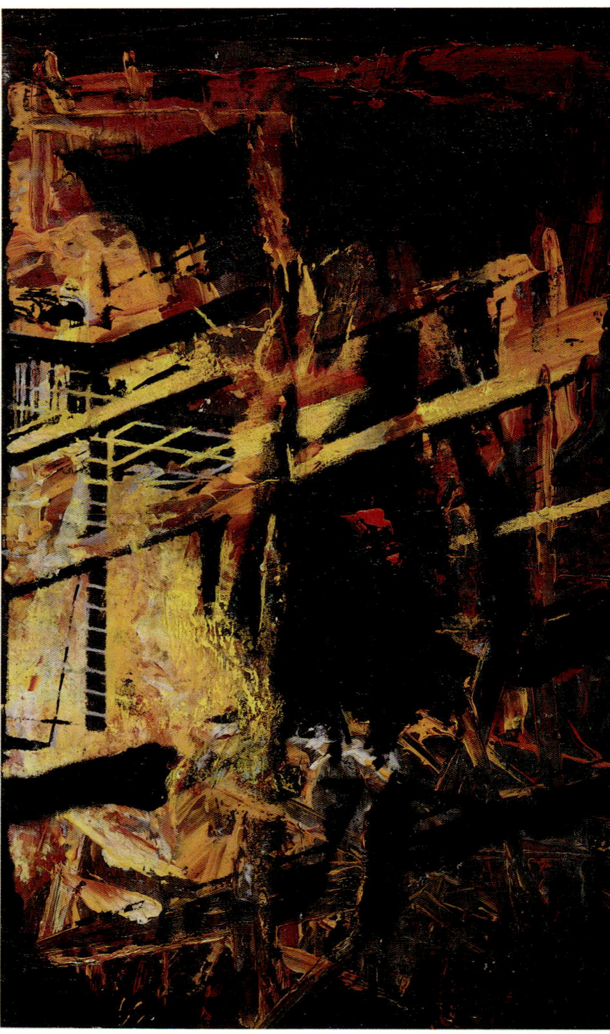

LIFE GOES ON III (LIVERPOOL ST) 1990

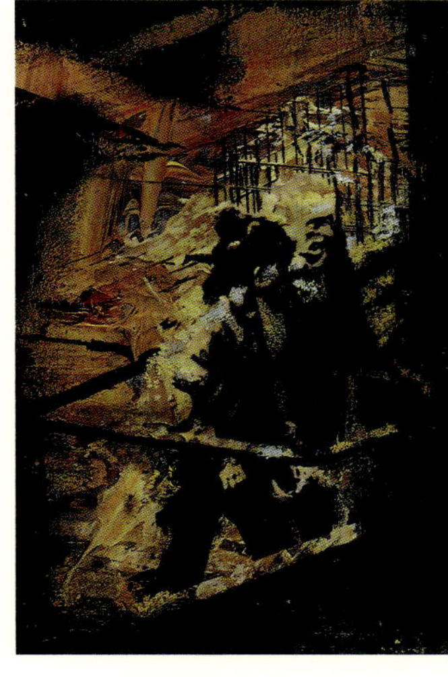
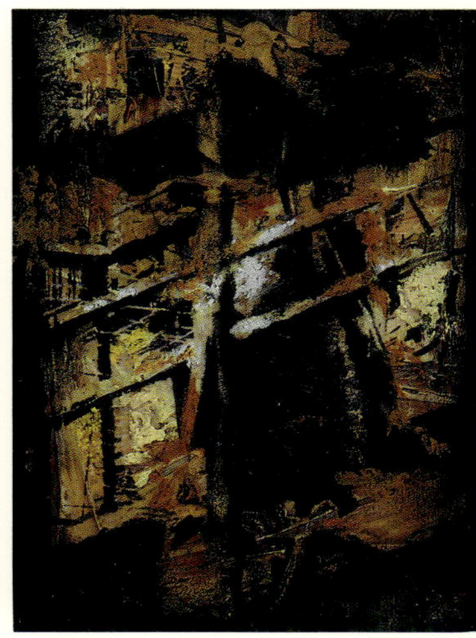
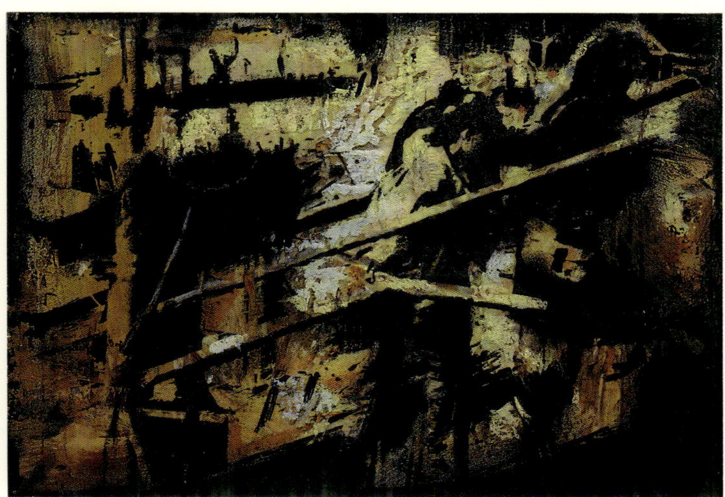
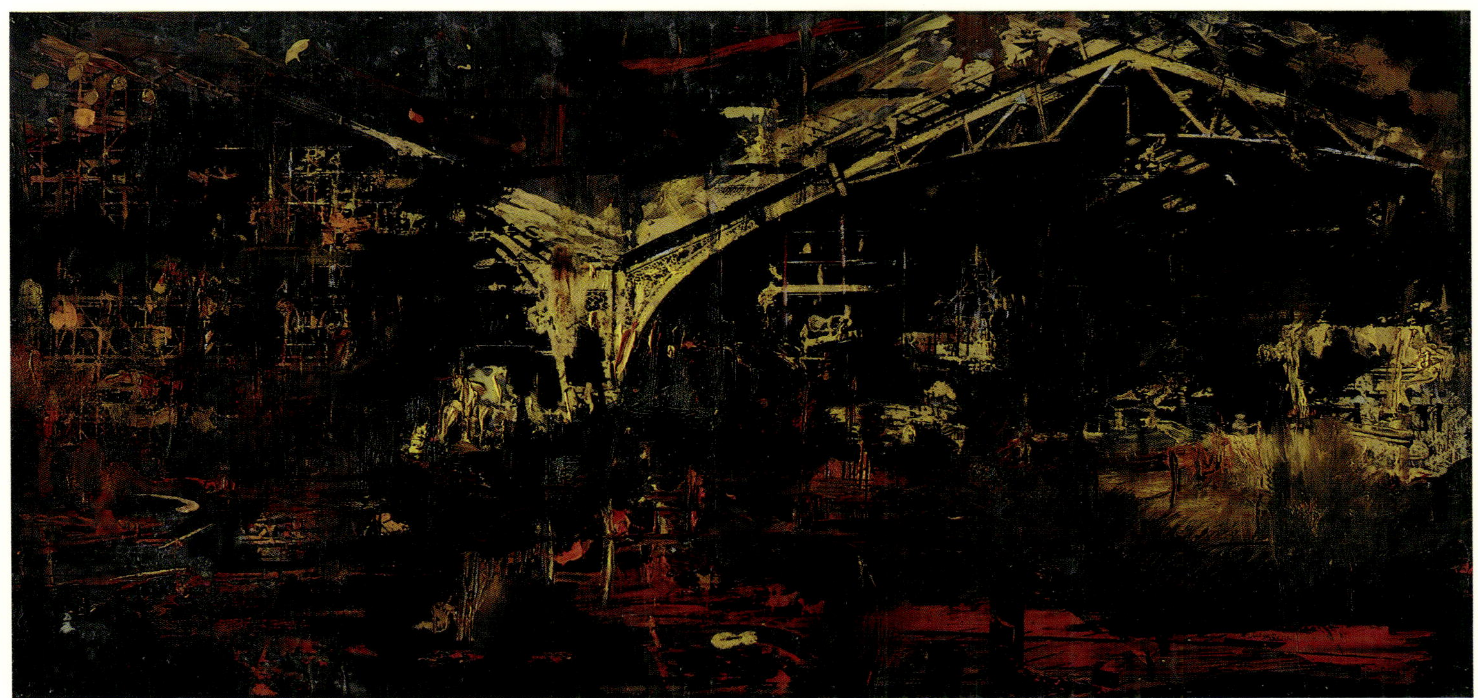

LIFE GOES ON, LIVERPOOL ST I 1989

LIVERPOOL ST STATION UNDER CONSTRUCTION 1989

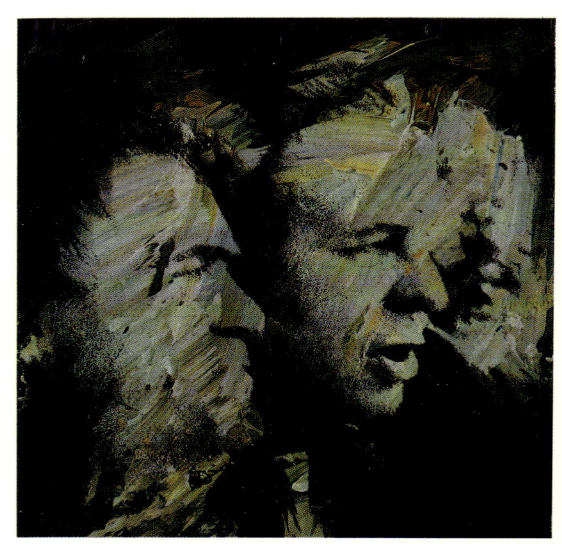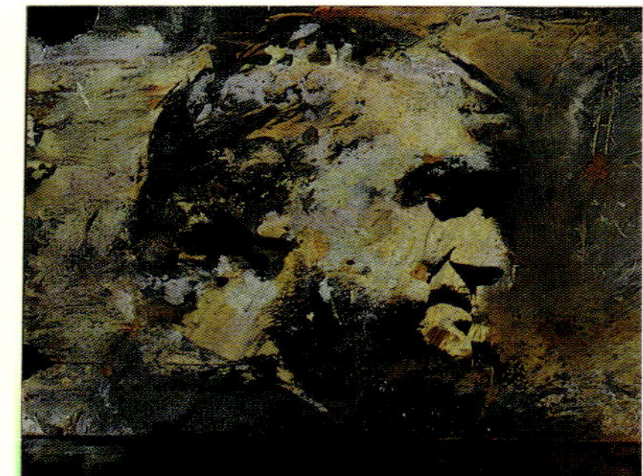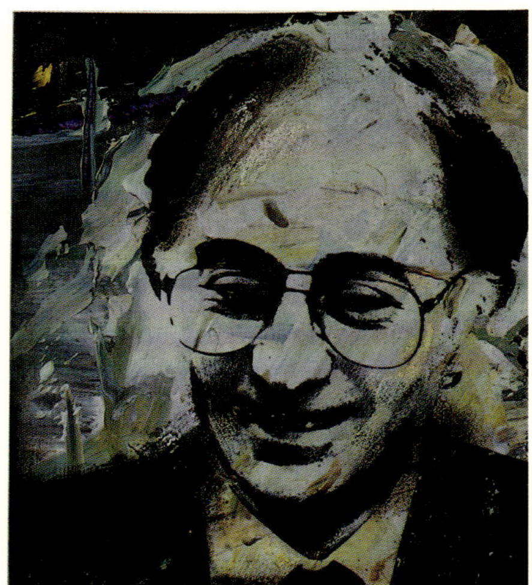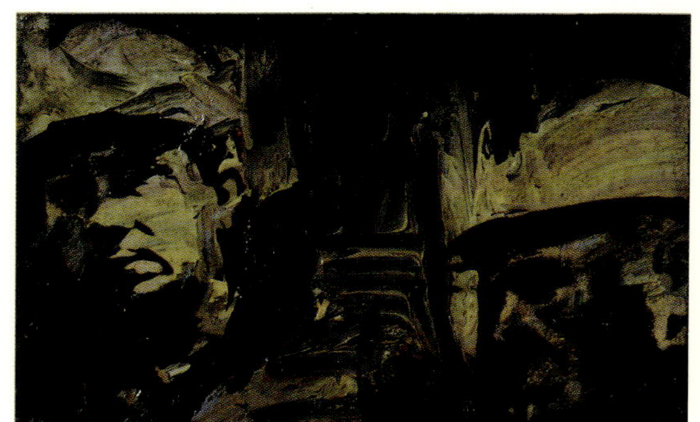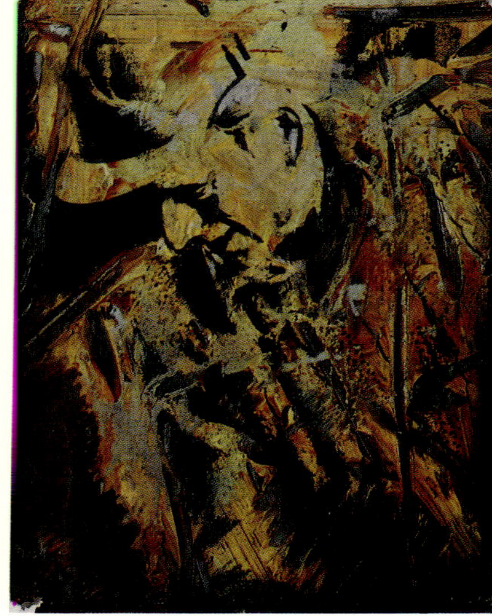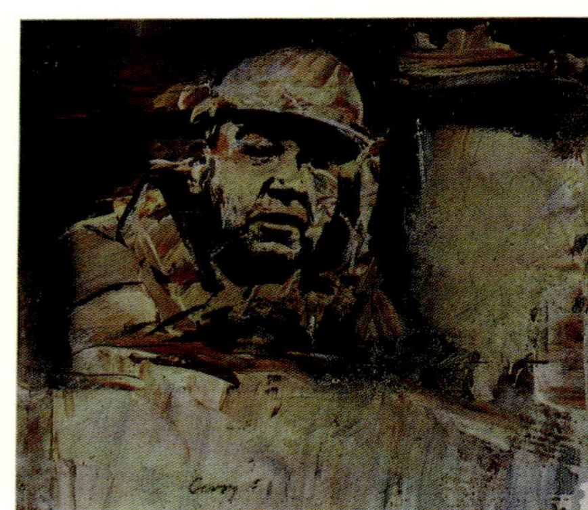

HEADS 1989-90

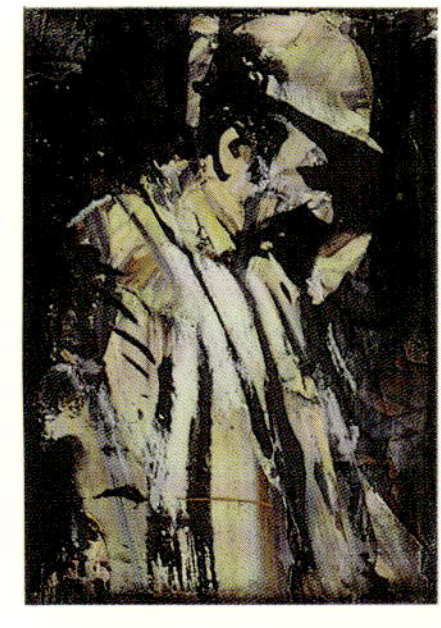
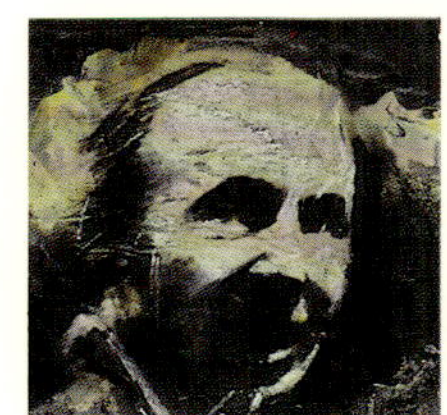
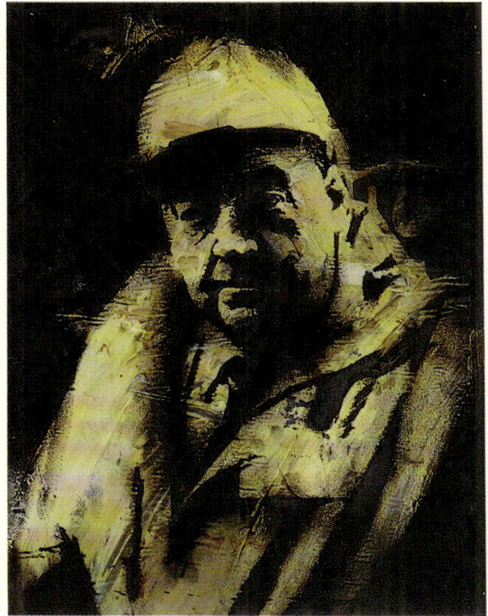
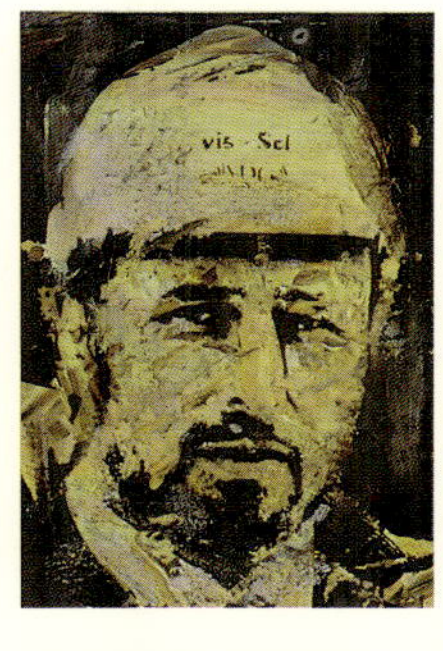
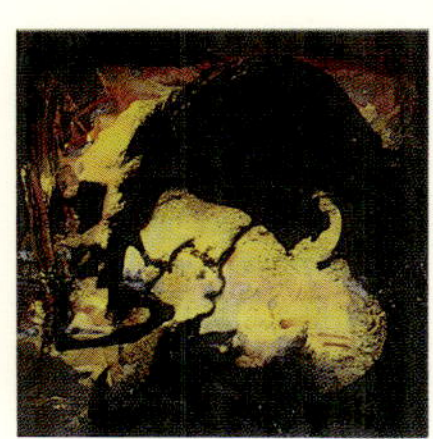
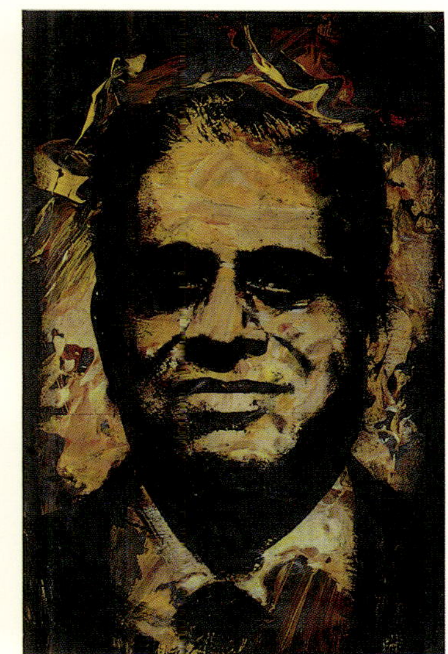
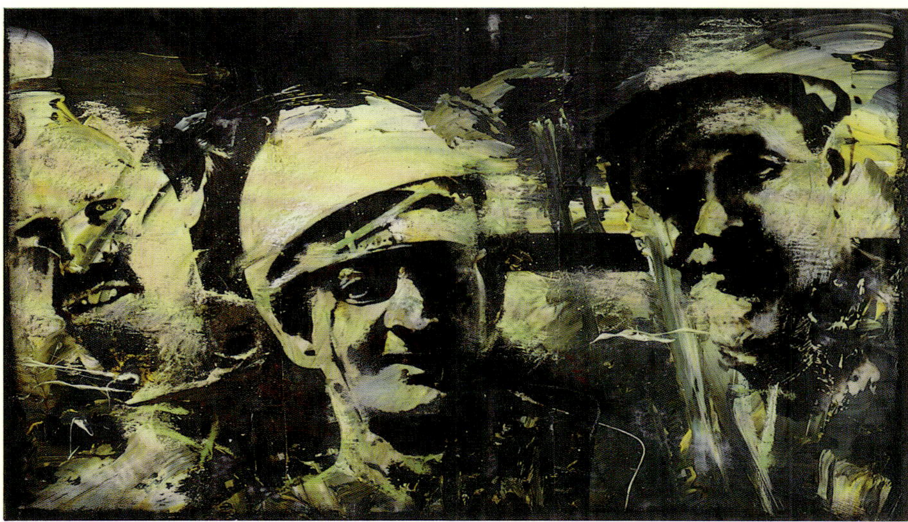
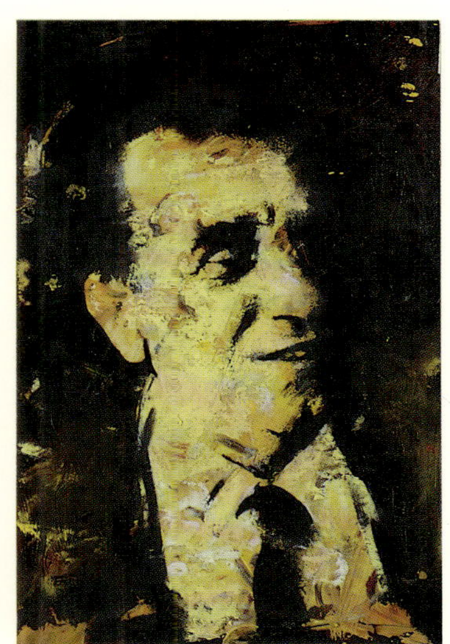
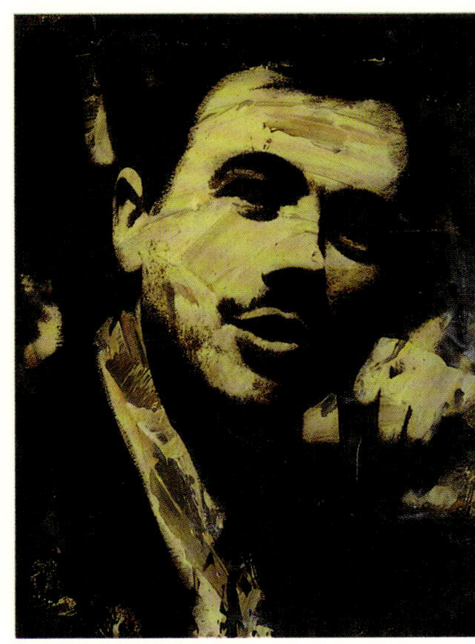
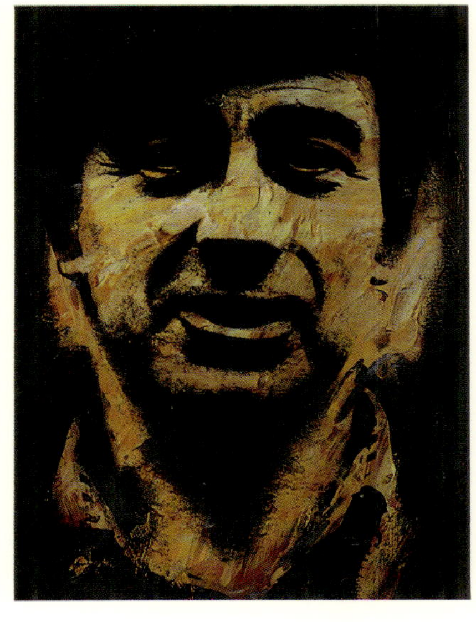
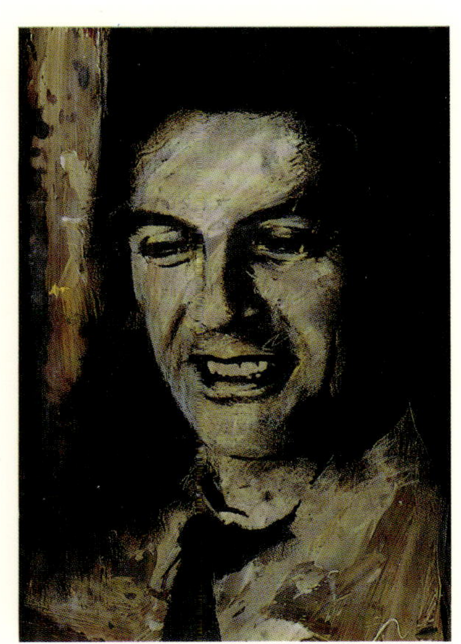

HEADS 1989

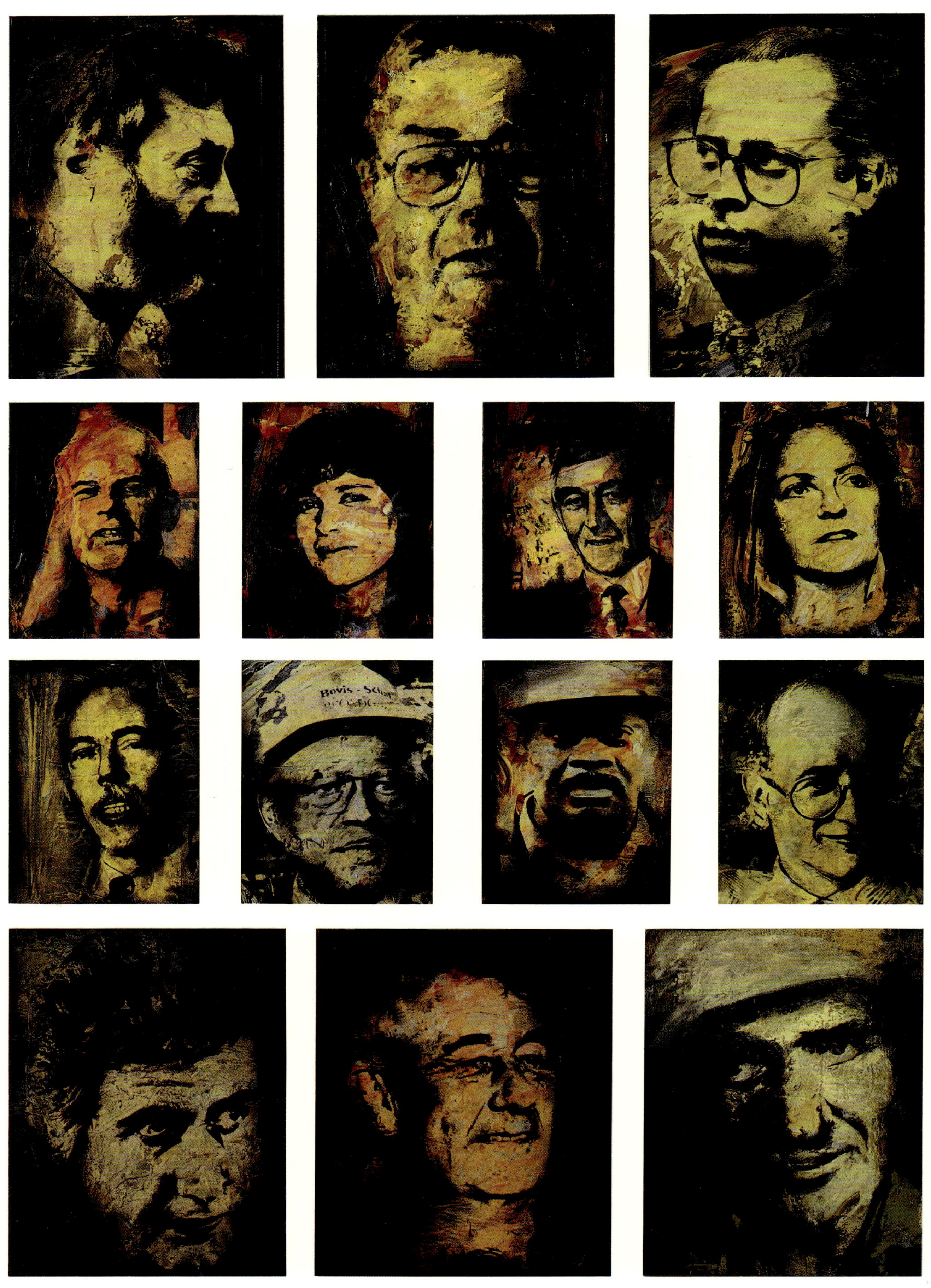

HEADS 1989-90

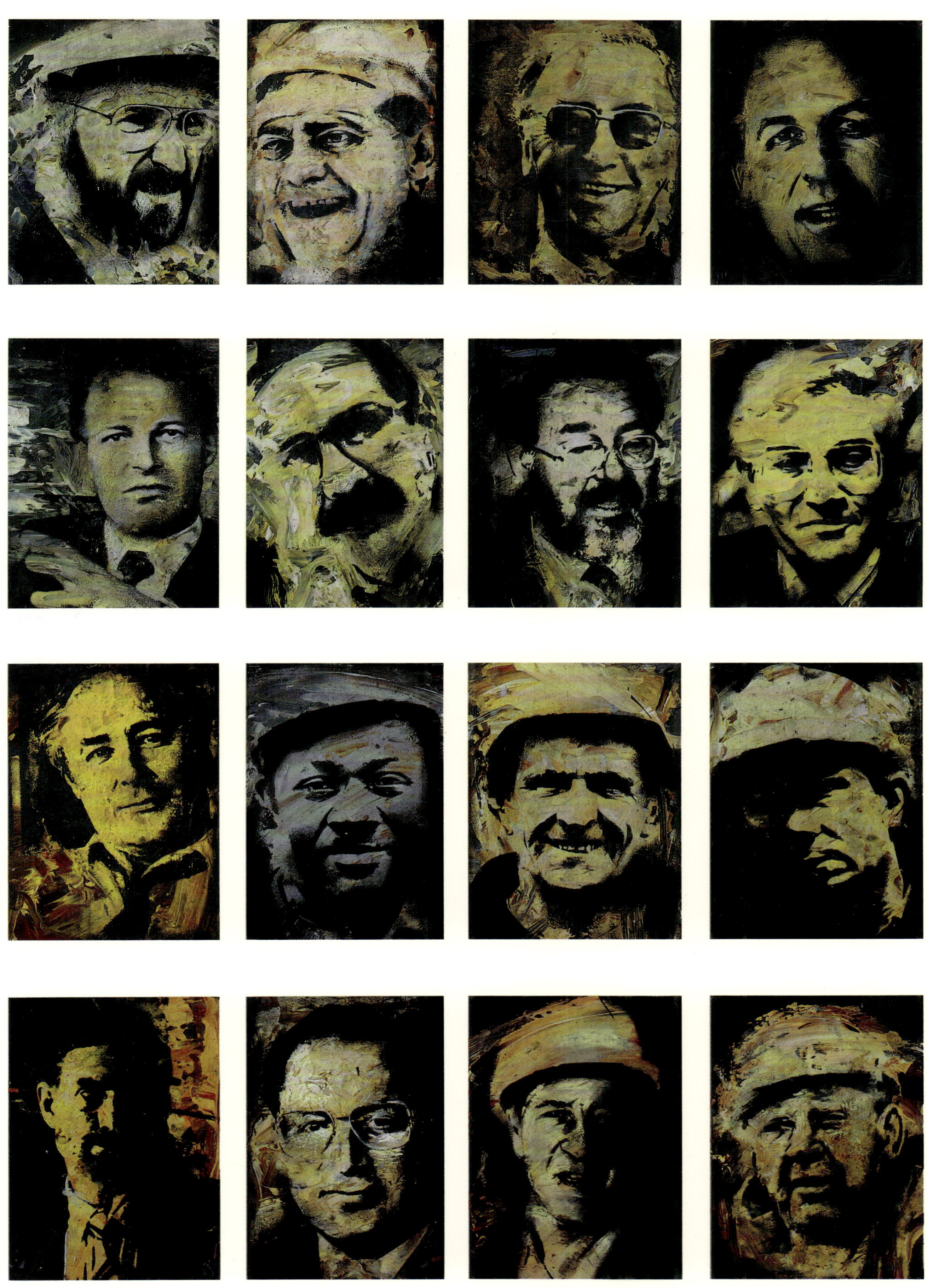

HEADS 1989-90

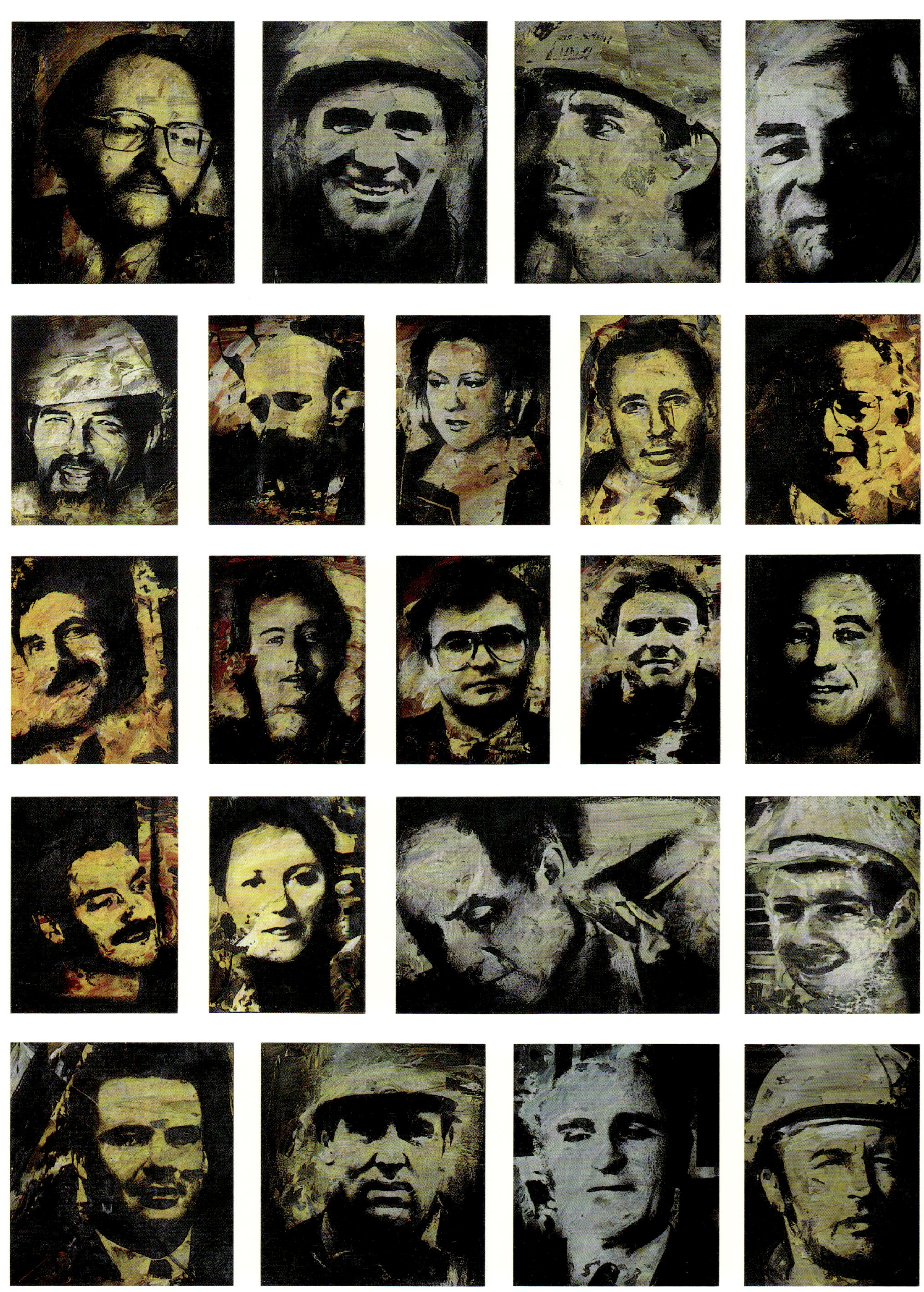

HEADS 1989-90

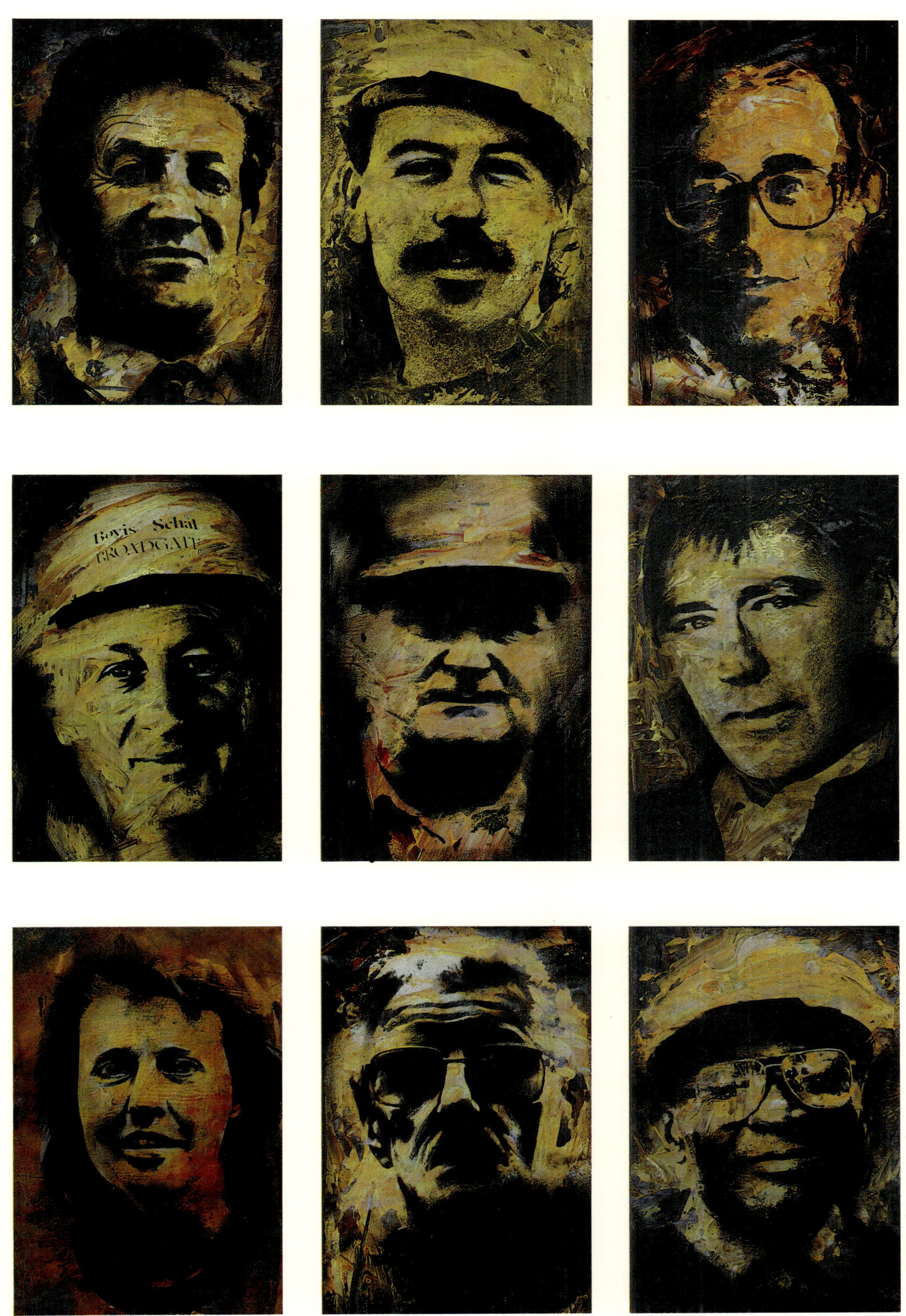

HEADS 1989-90

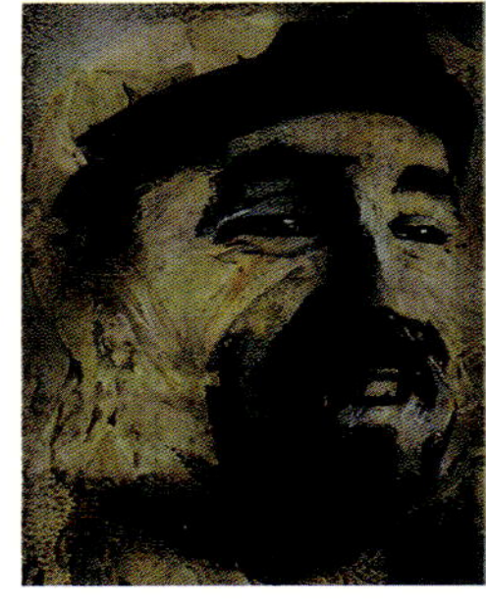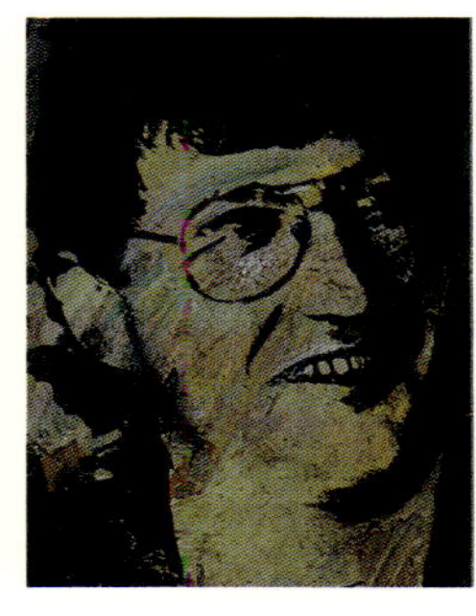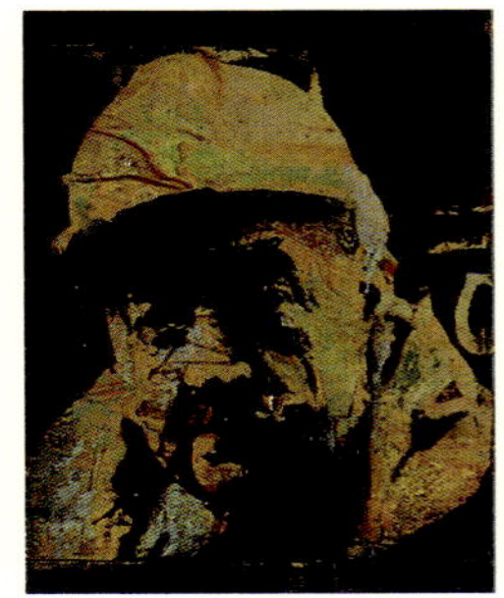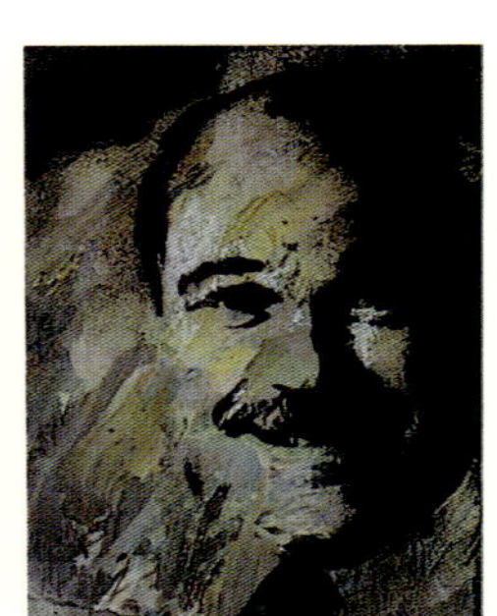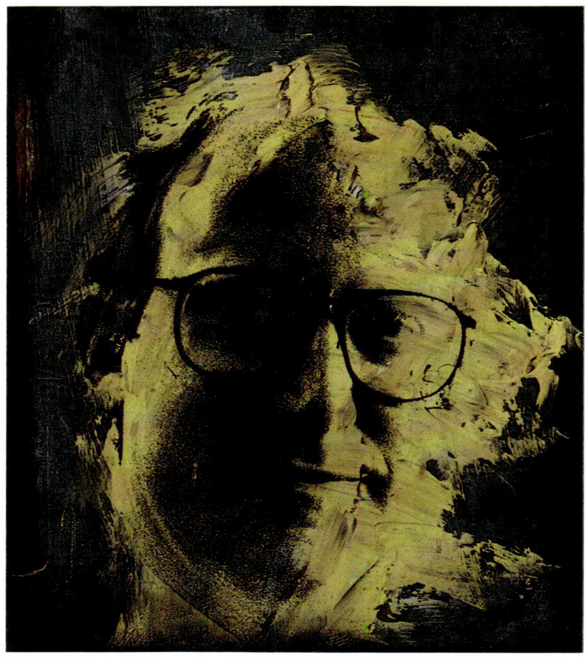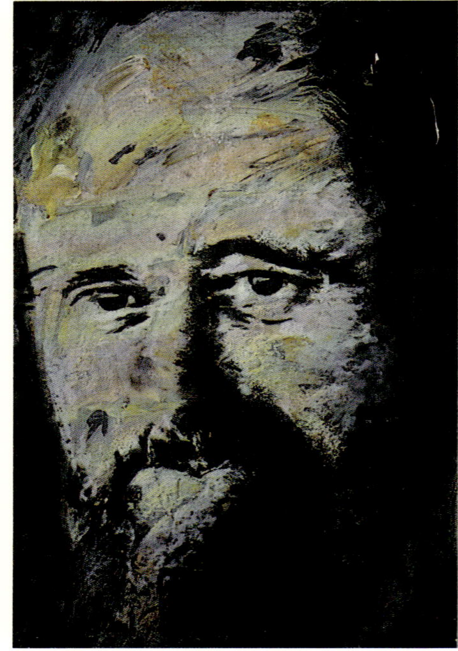

HEADS 1989

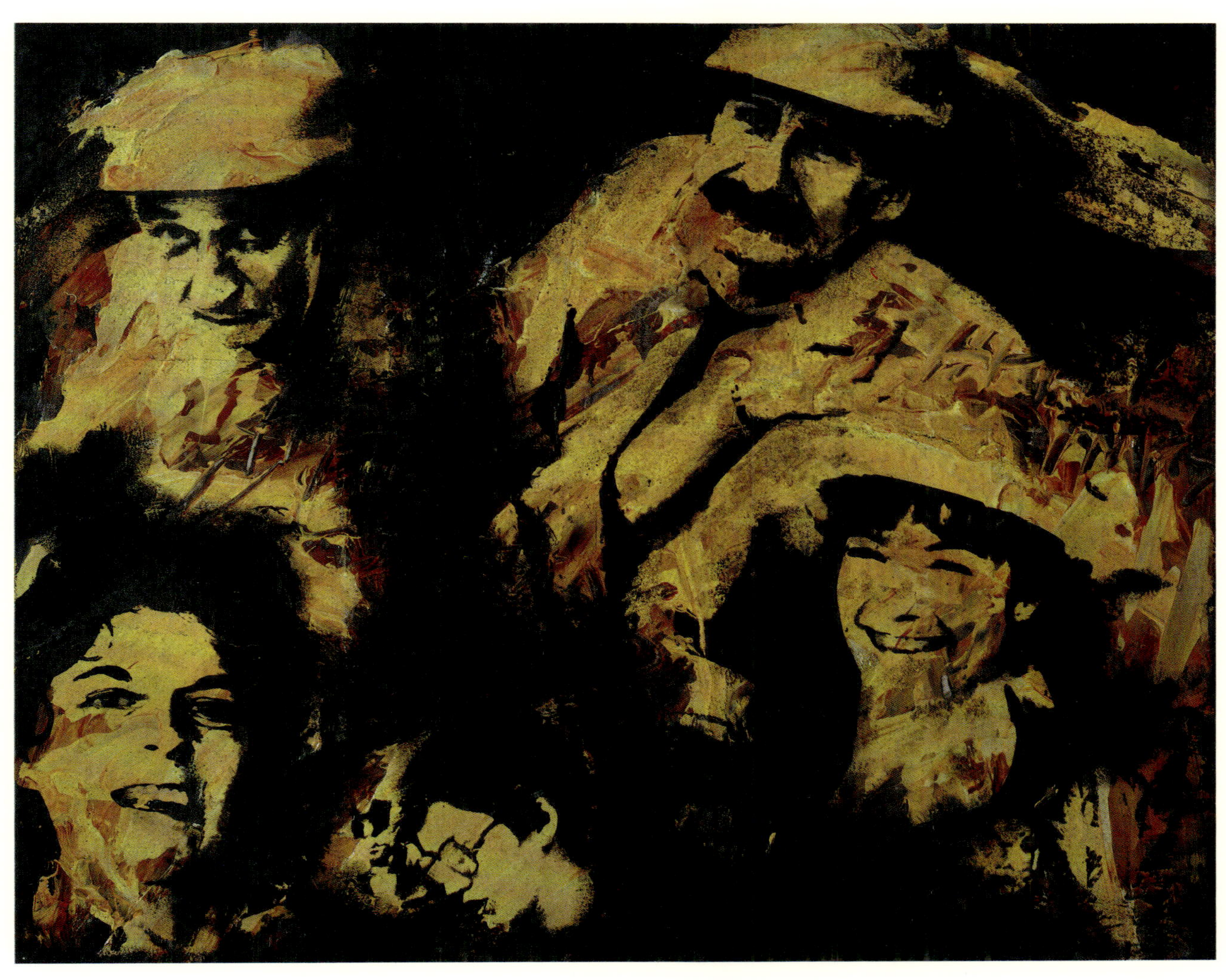

GROUP PICTURE WITH FREIDA, CHRISTINE AND OTHERS 1989

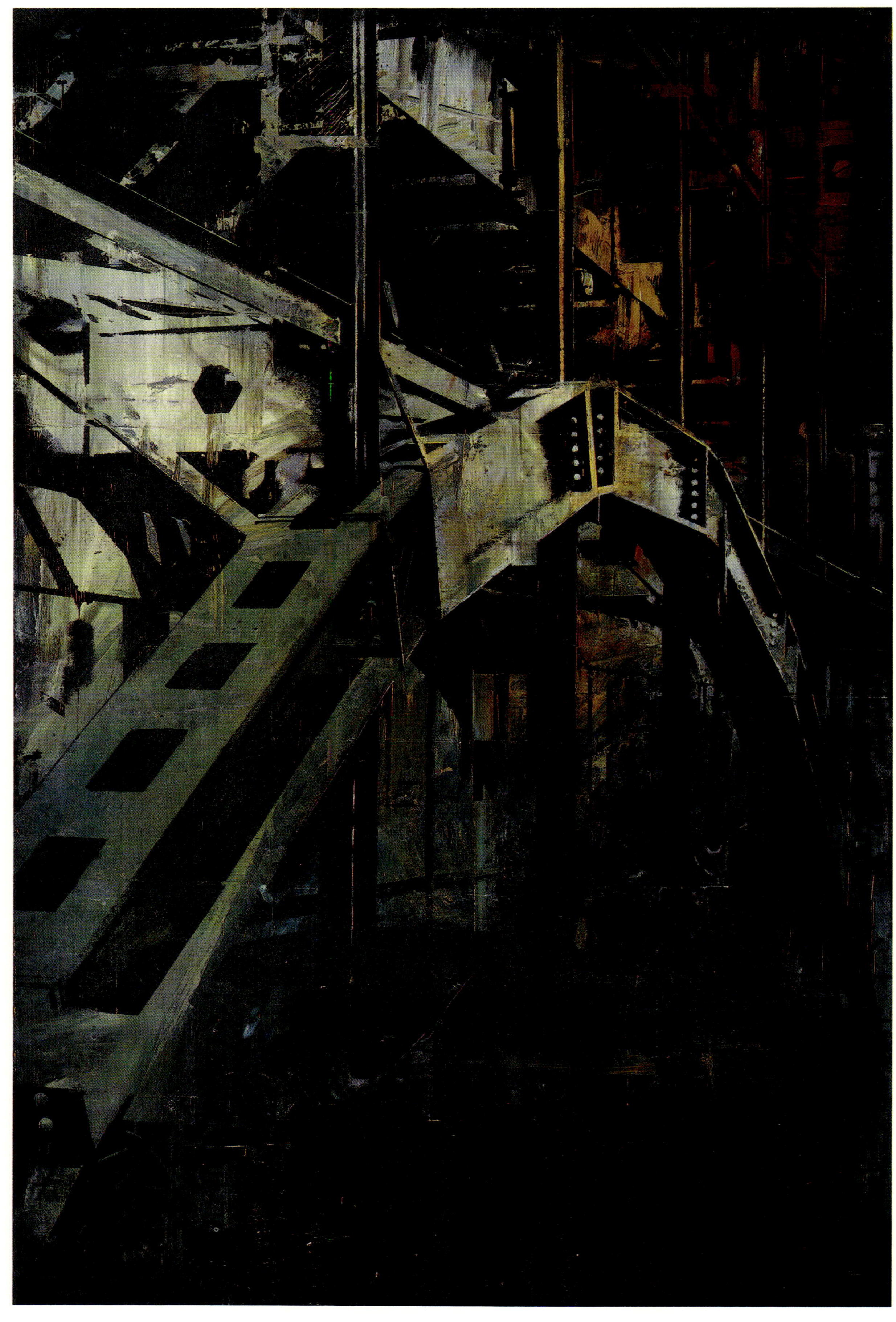

PHASE II 1989

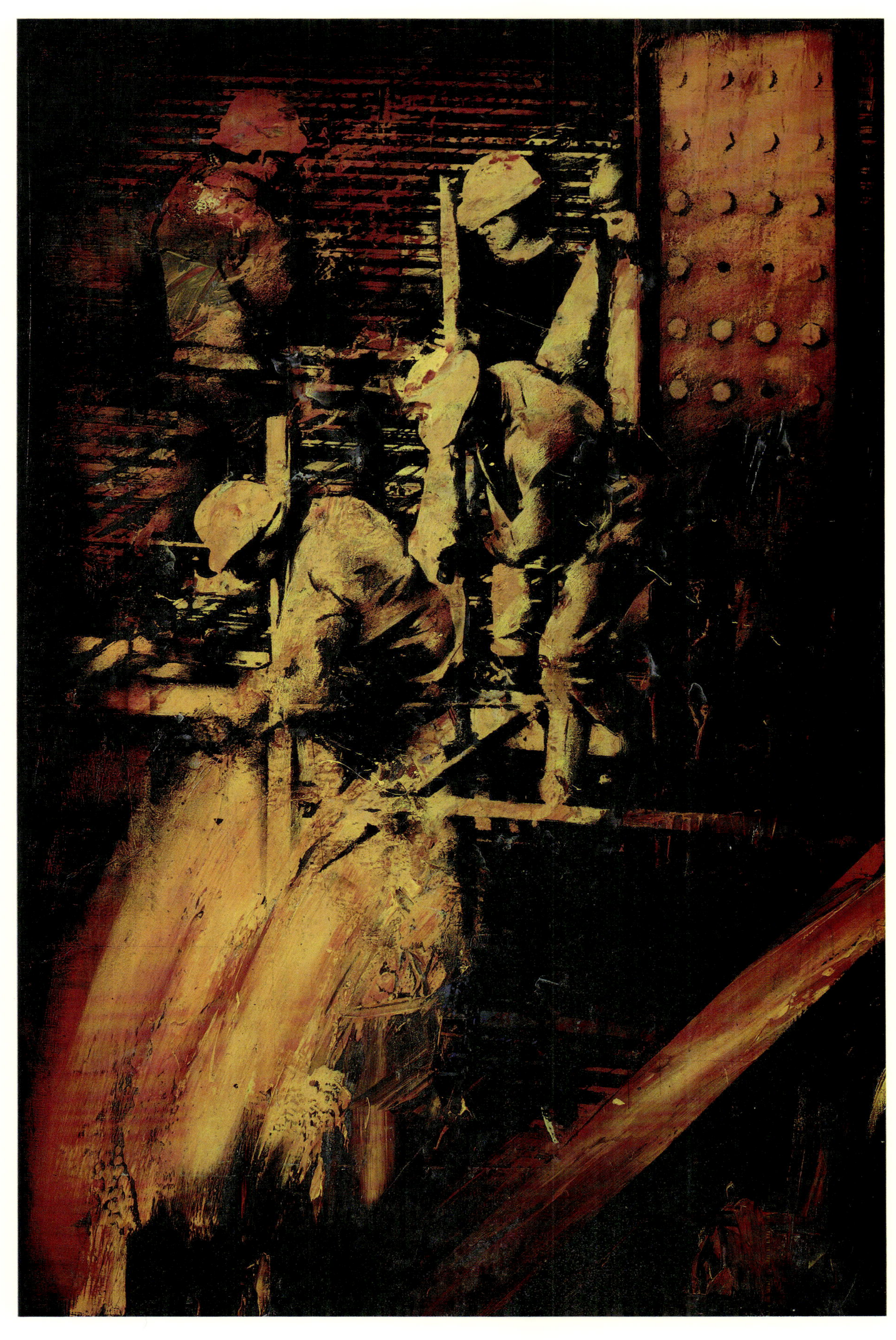

PHASE II (RAINY DAY) 1989

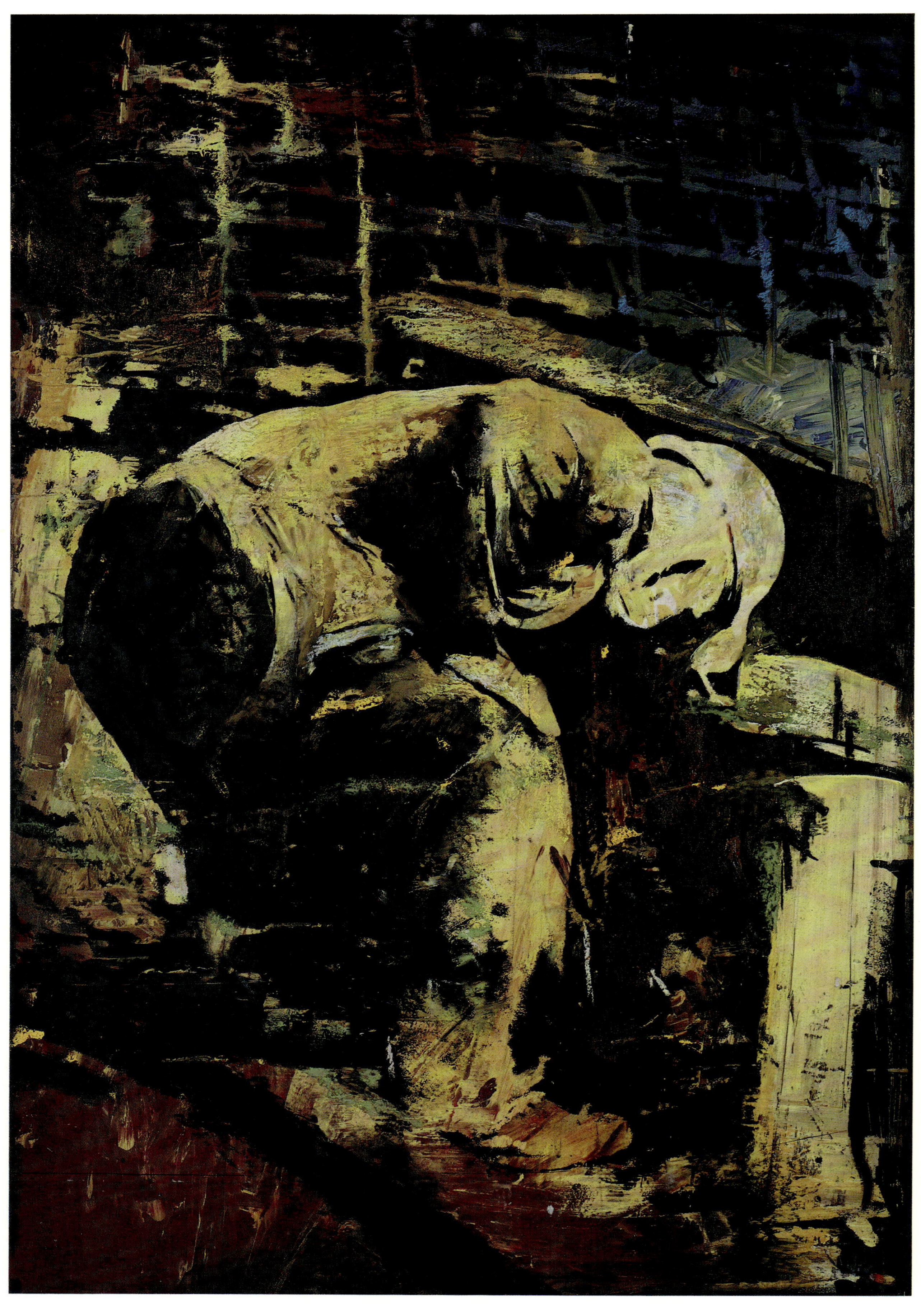

WORKER, NIGHTSHIFT 1989

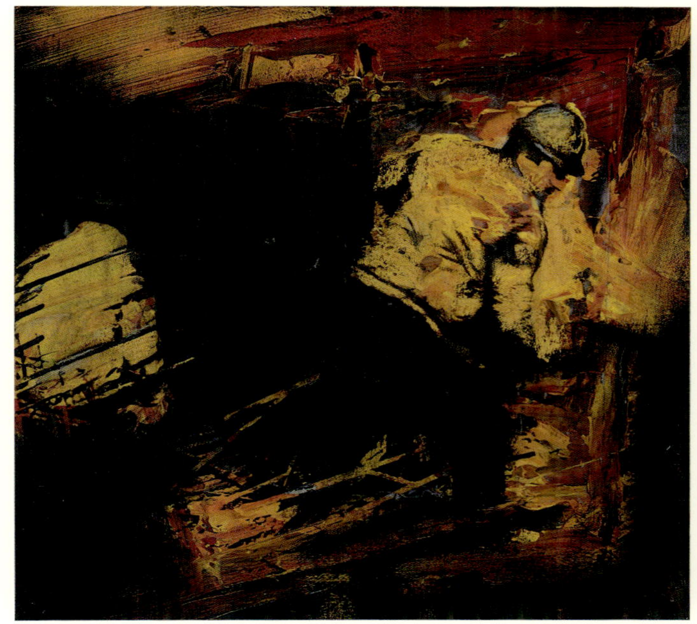 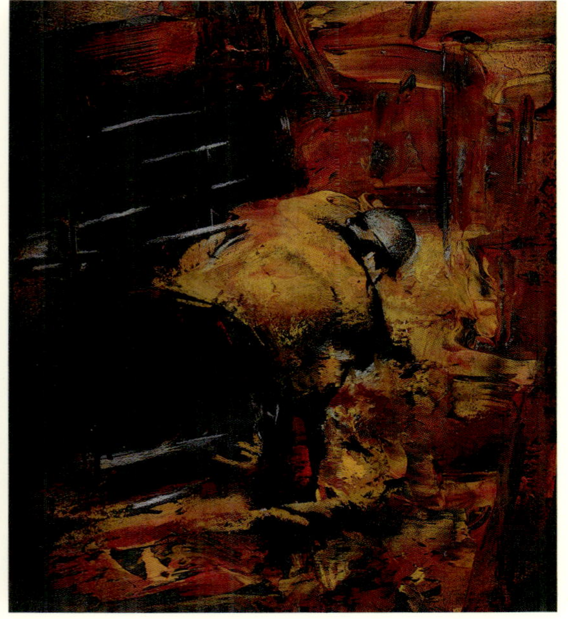

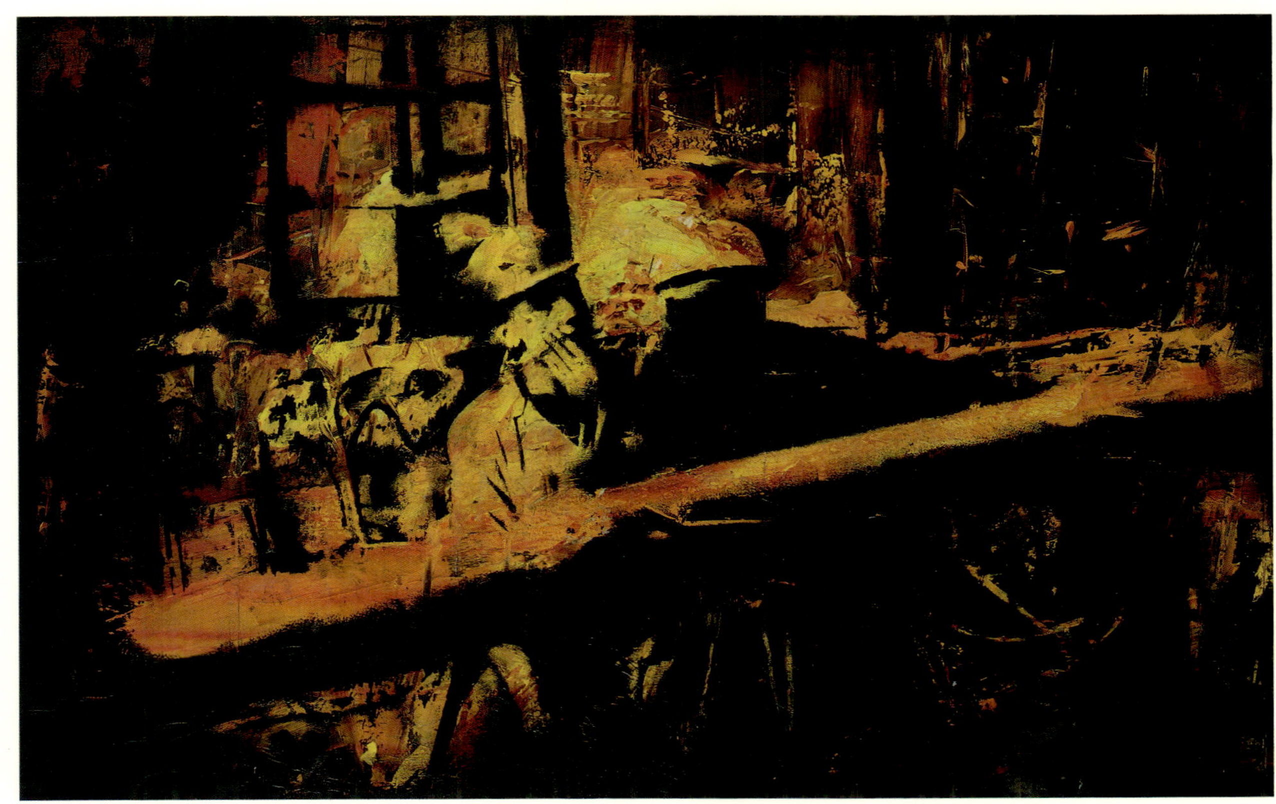

NIGHTSHIFT I. BROADGATE 1989   NIGHTSHIFT II. BROADGATE 1989
THE THINKER. BROADGATE 1989-90

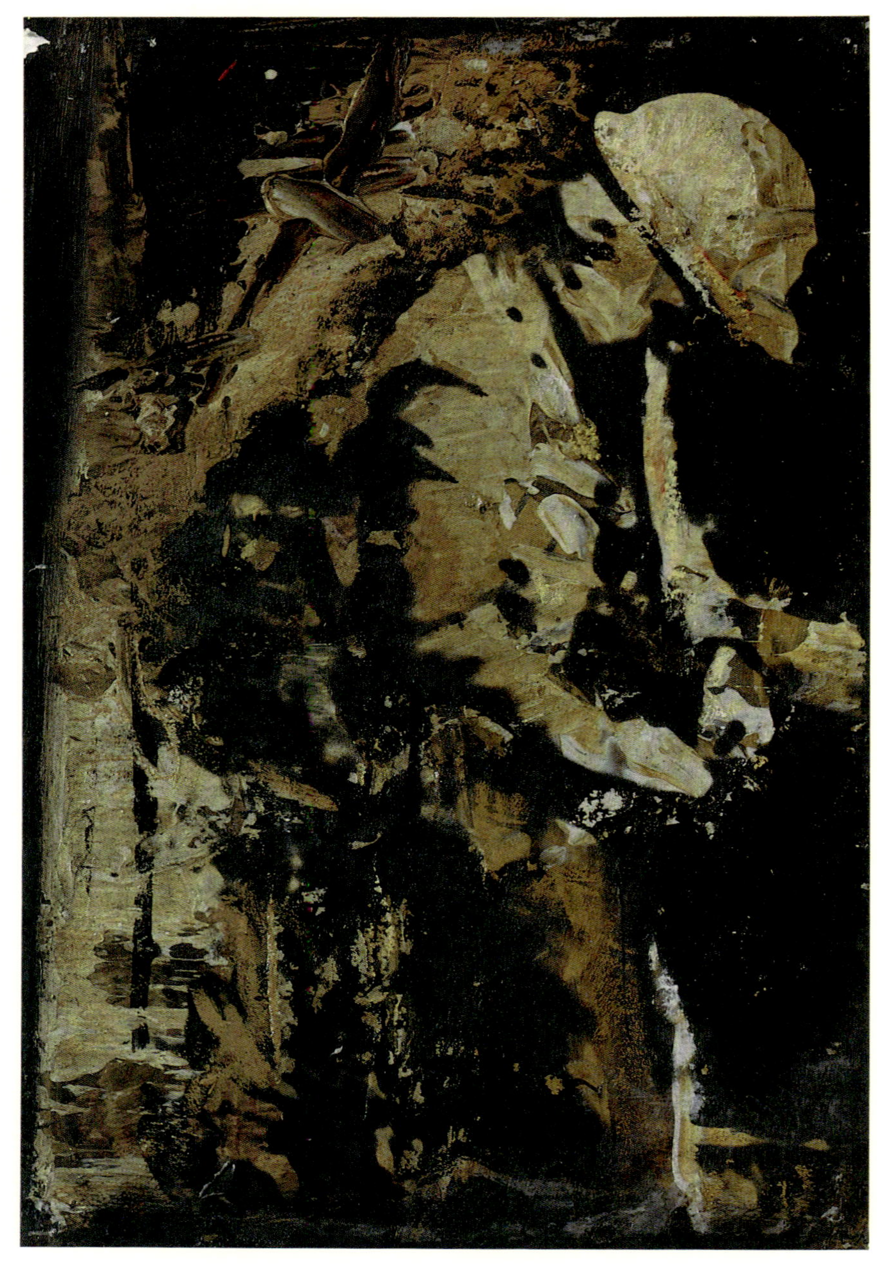

SKETCHBOOK STUDY 1989

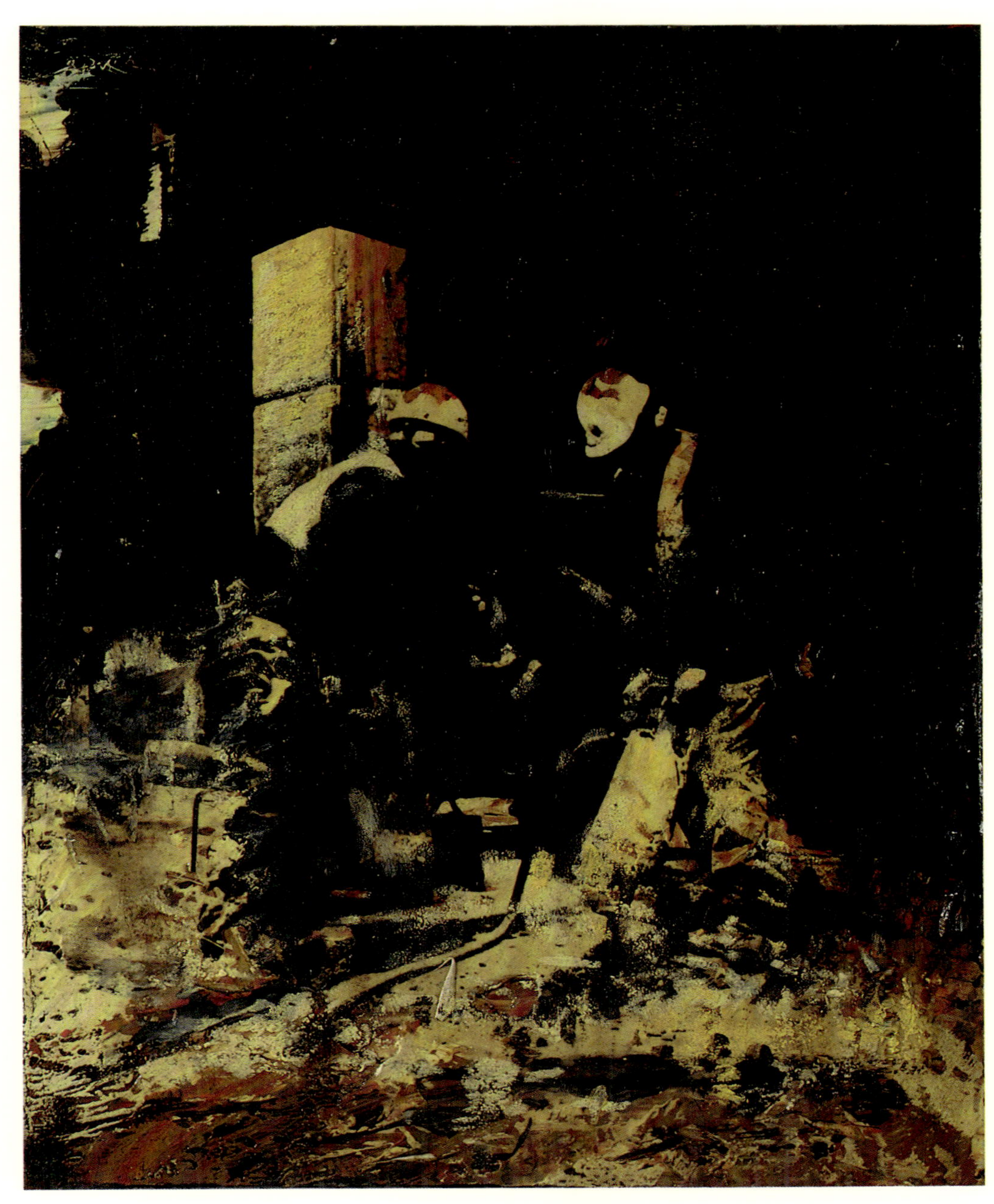

NIGHT WORK 1989

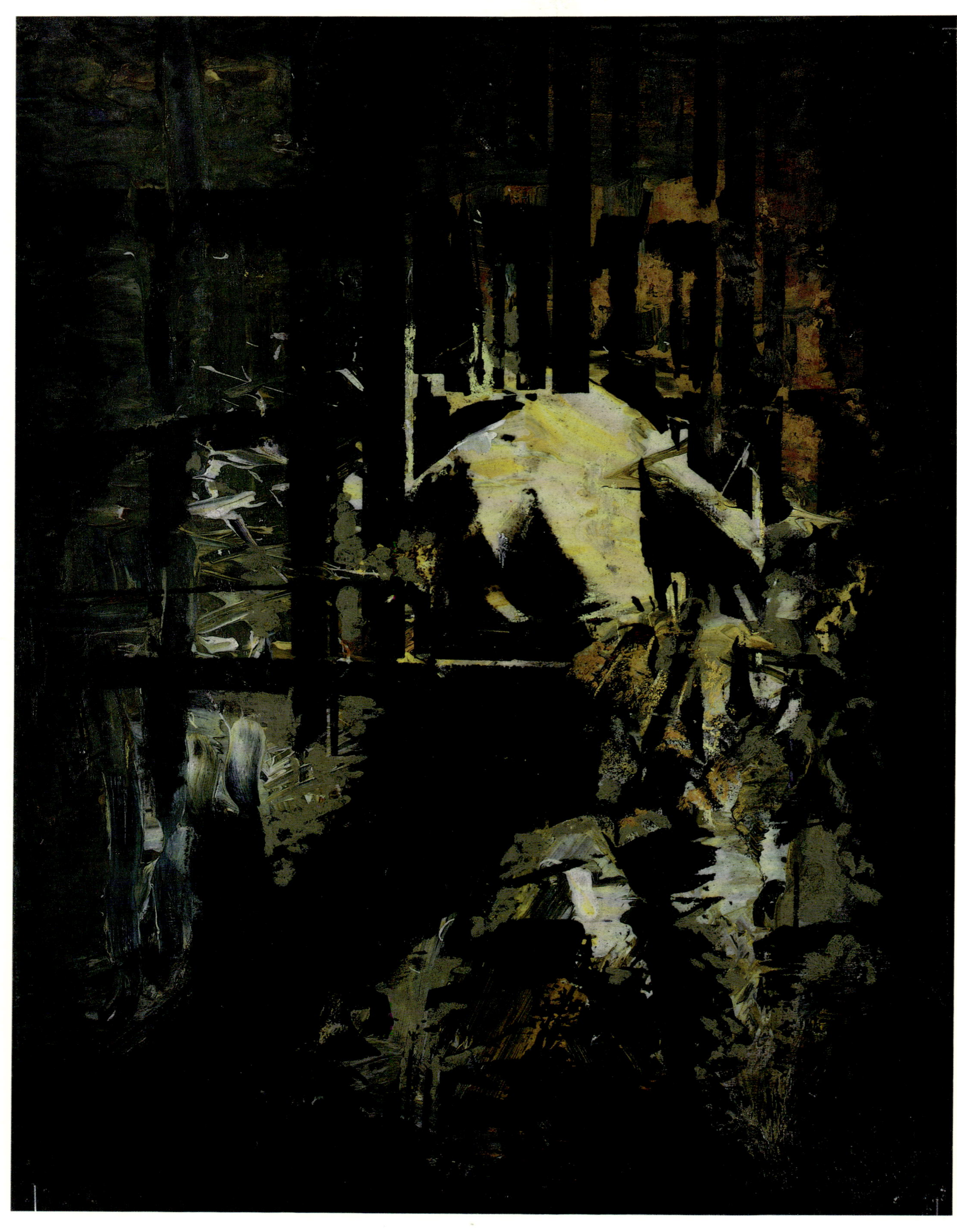

STUDY FOR PAINTING 1989

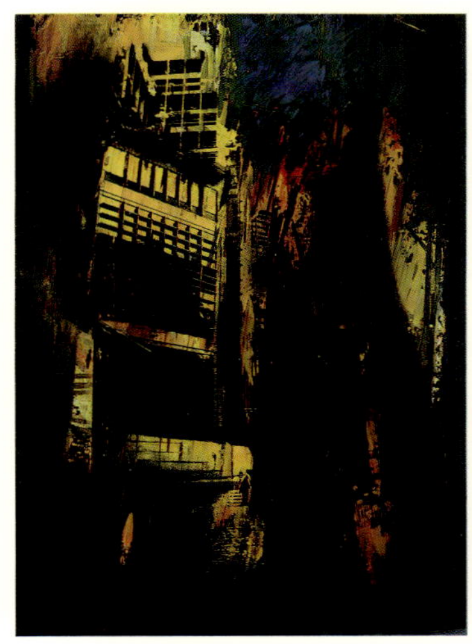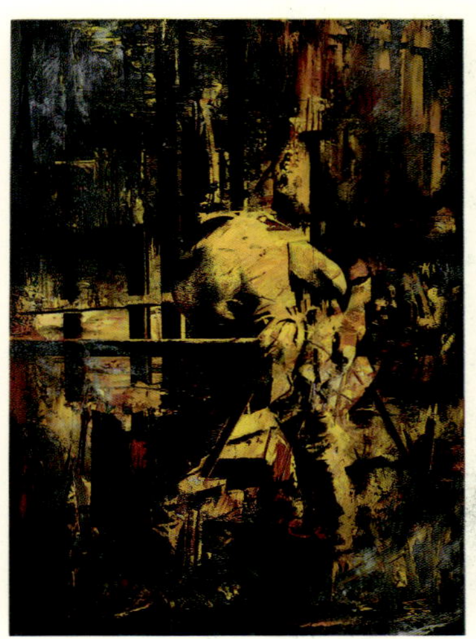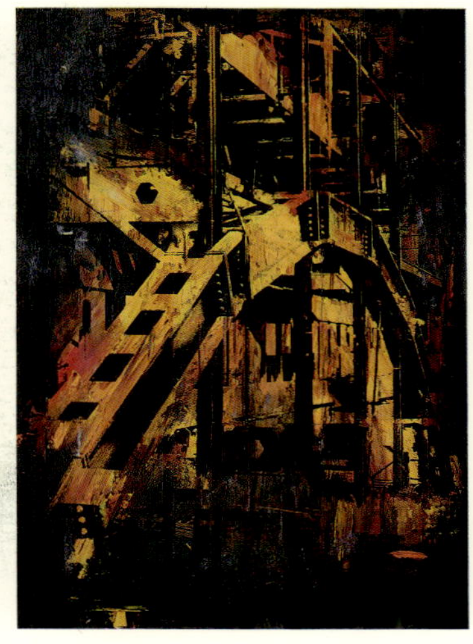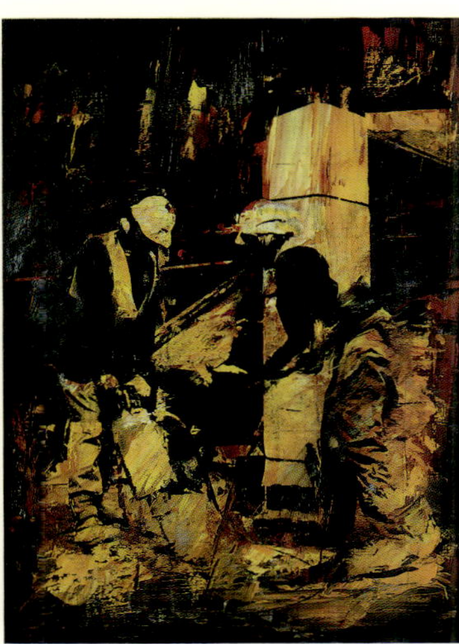

NIGHT AND DAY 1989

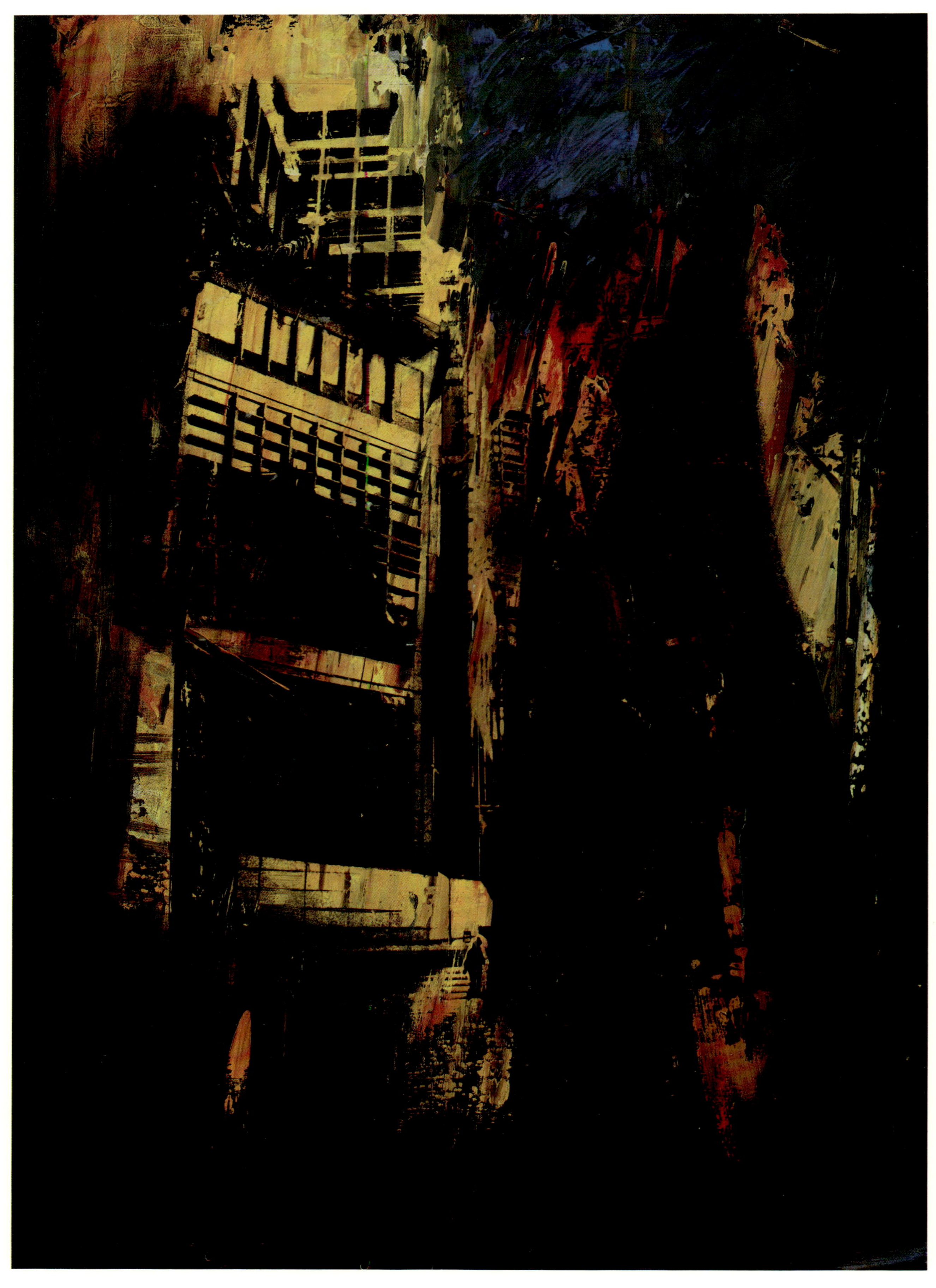

NIGHT AND DAY (FIRST PANEL) 1989

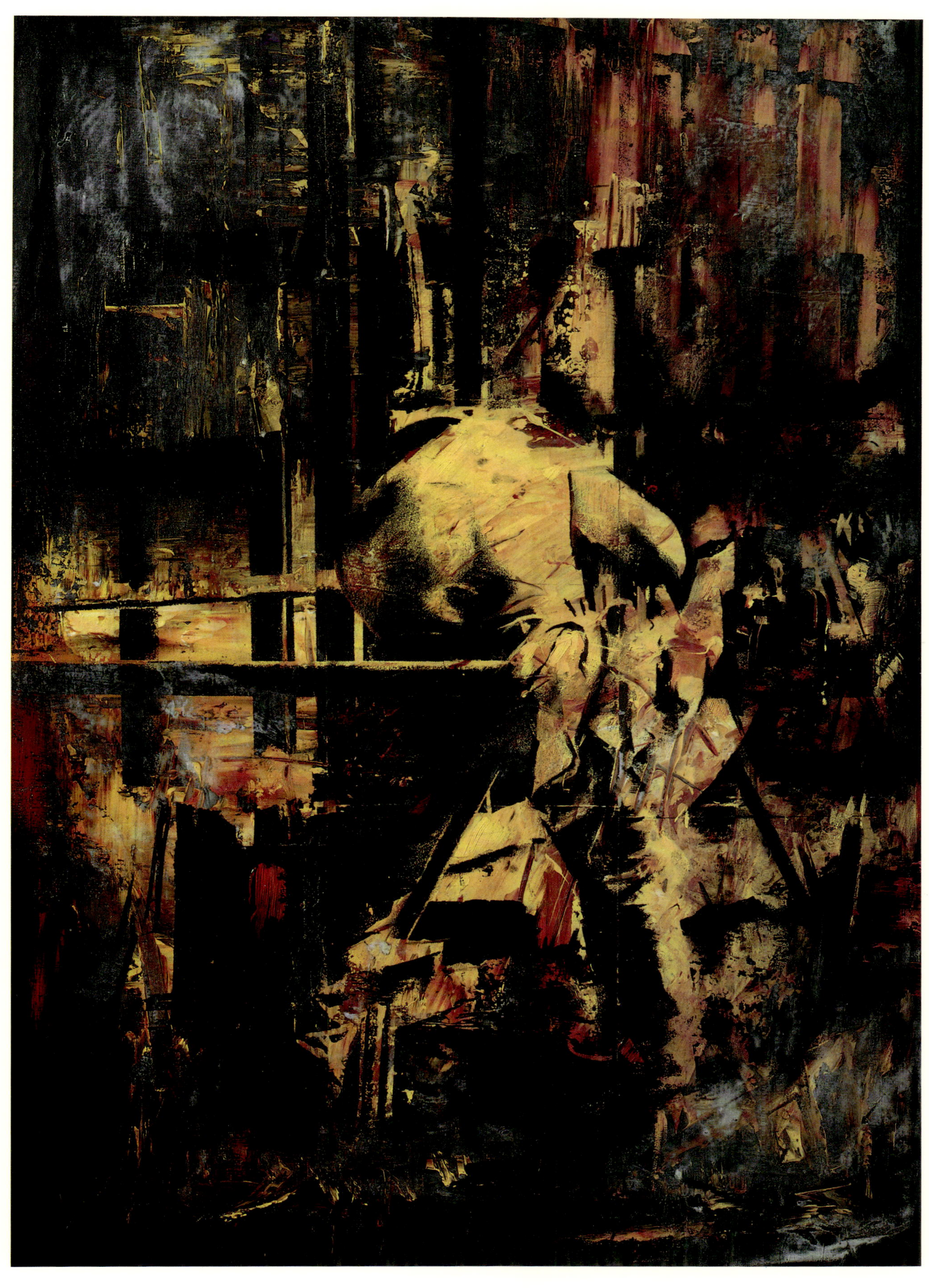

NIGHT AND DAY (SECOND PANEL) 1989

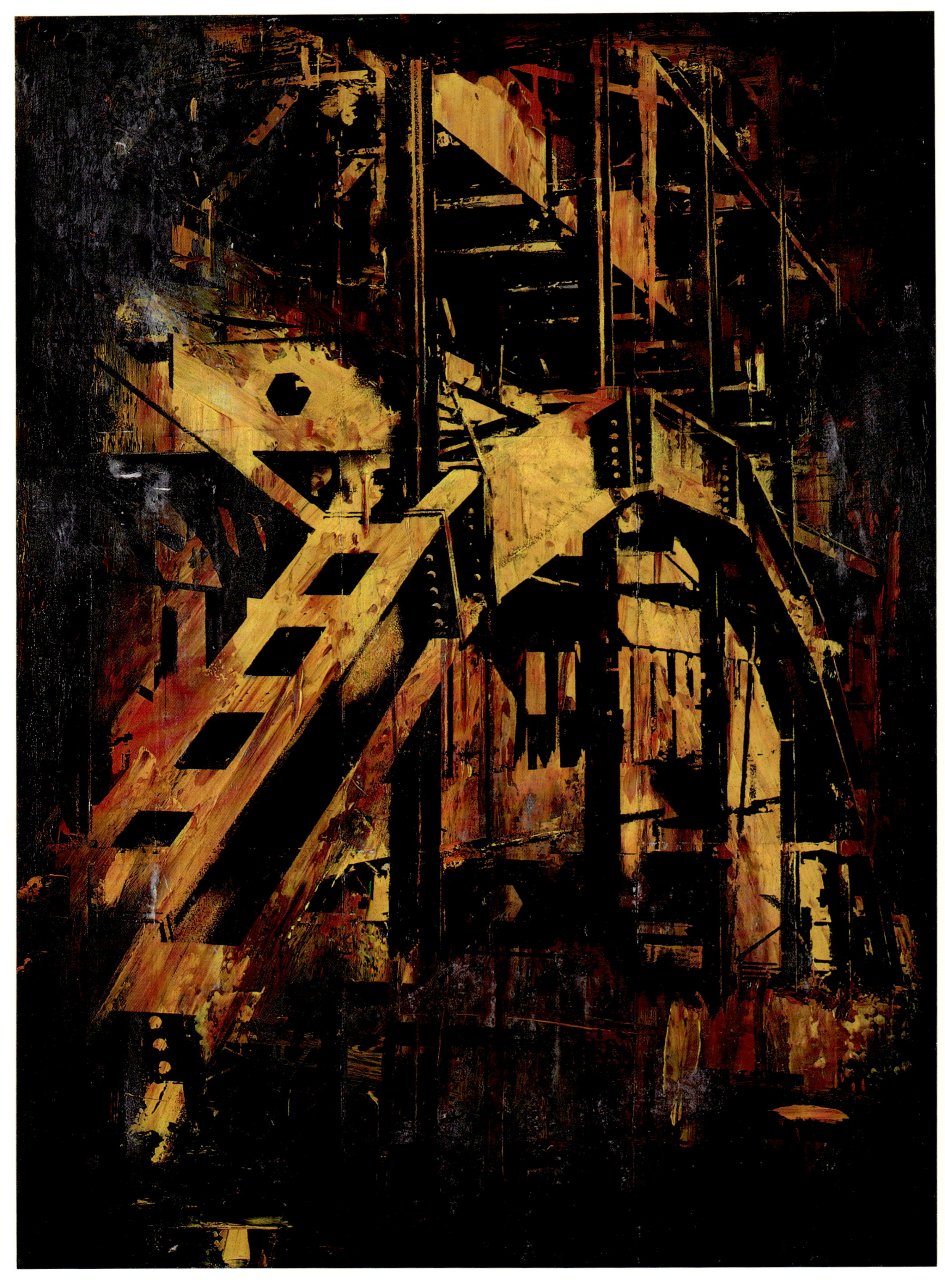

NIGHT AND DAY (THIRD PANEL) 1989

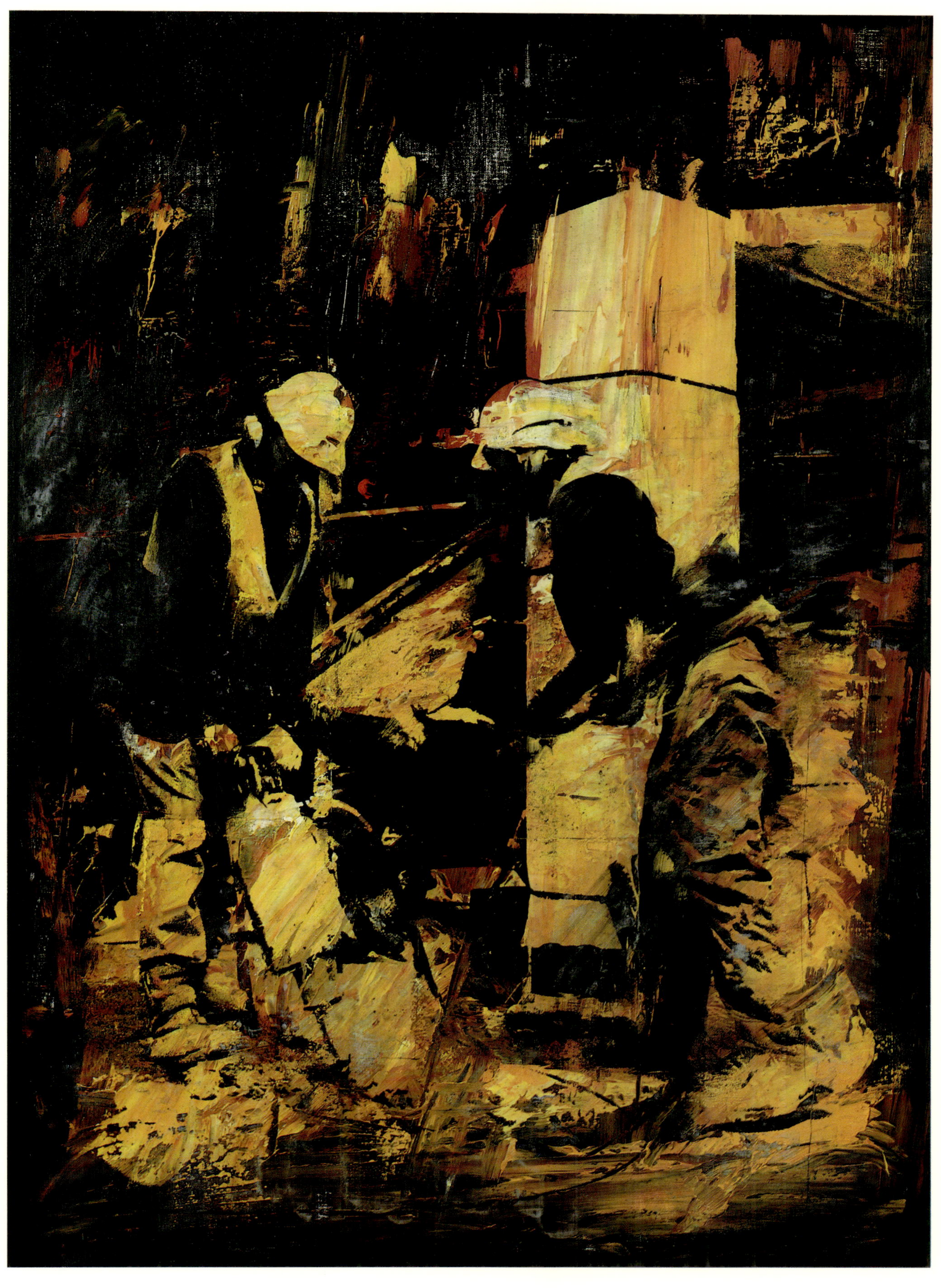

NIGHT AND DAY (FOURTH PANEL) 1989

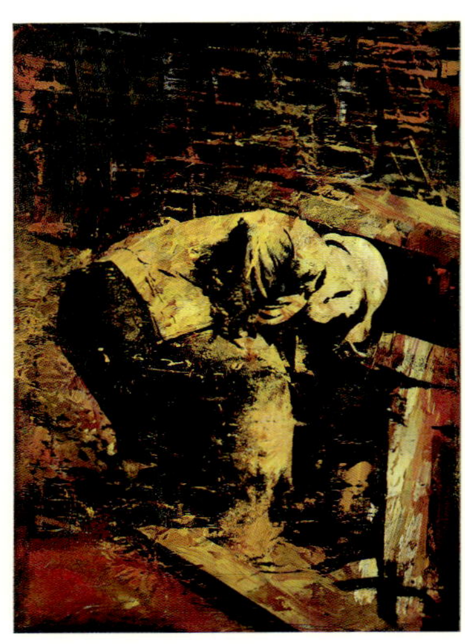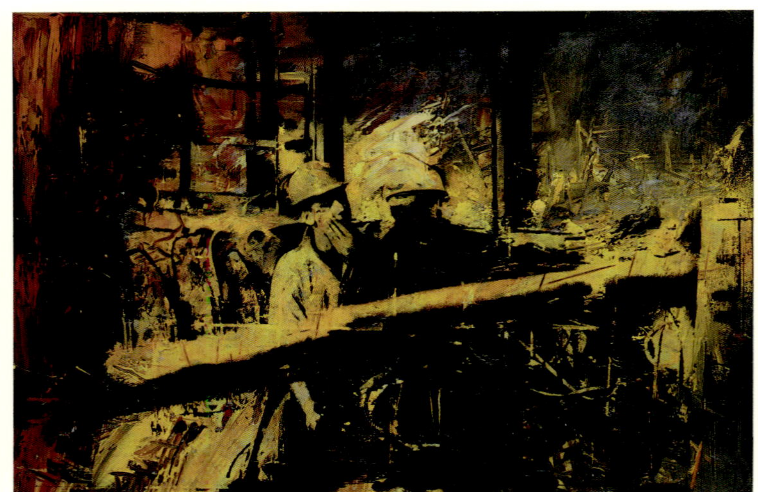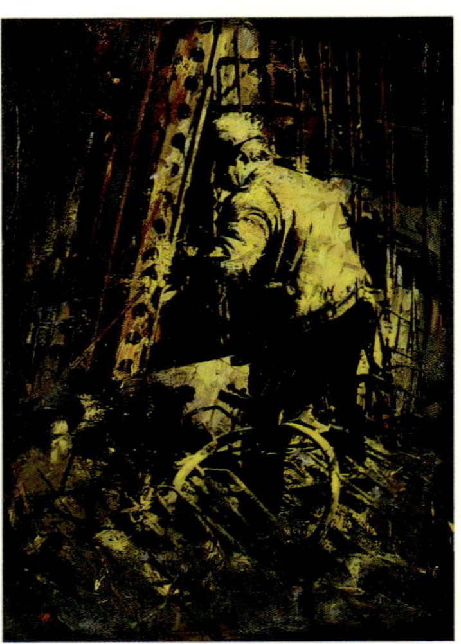

WORKERS BROADGATE 1989-90

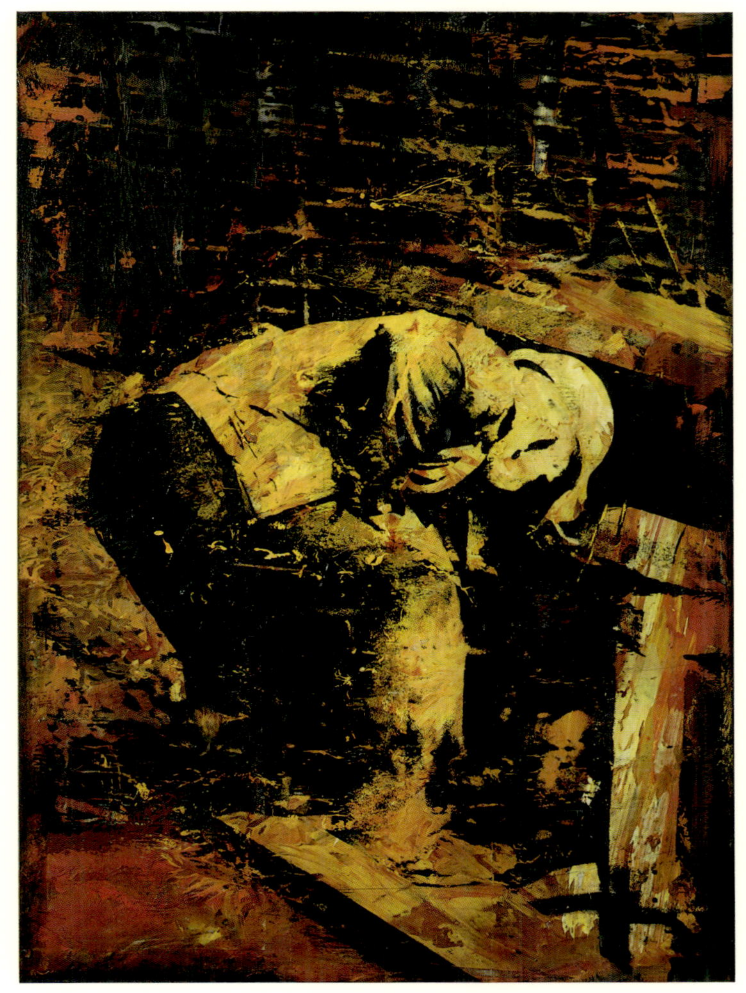

WORKERS BROADGATE (LEFT PANEL) 1989-90

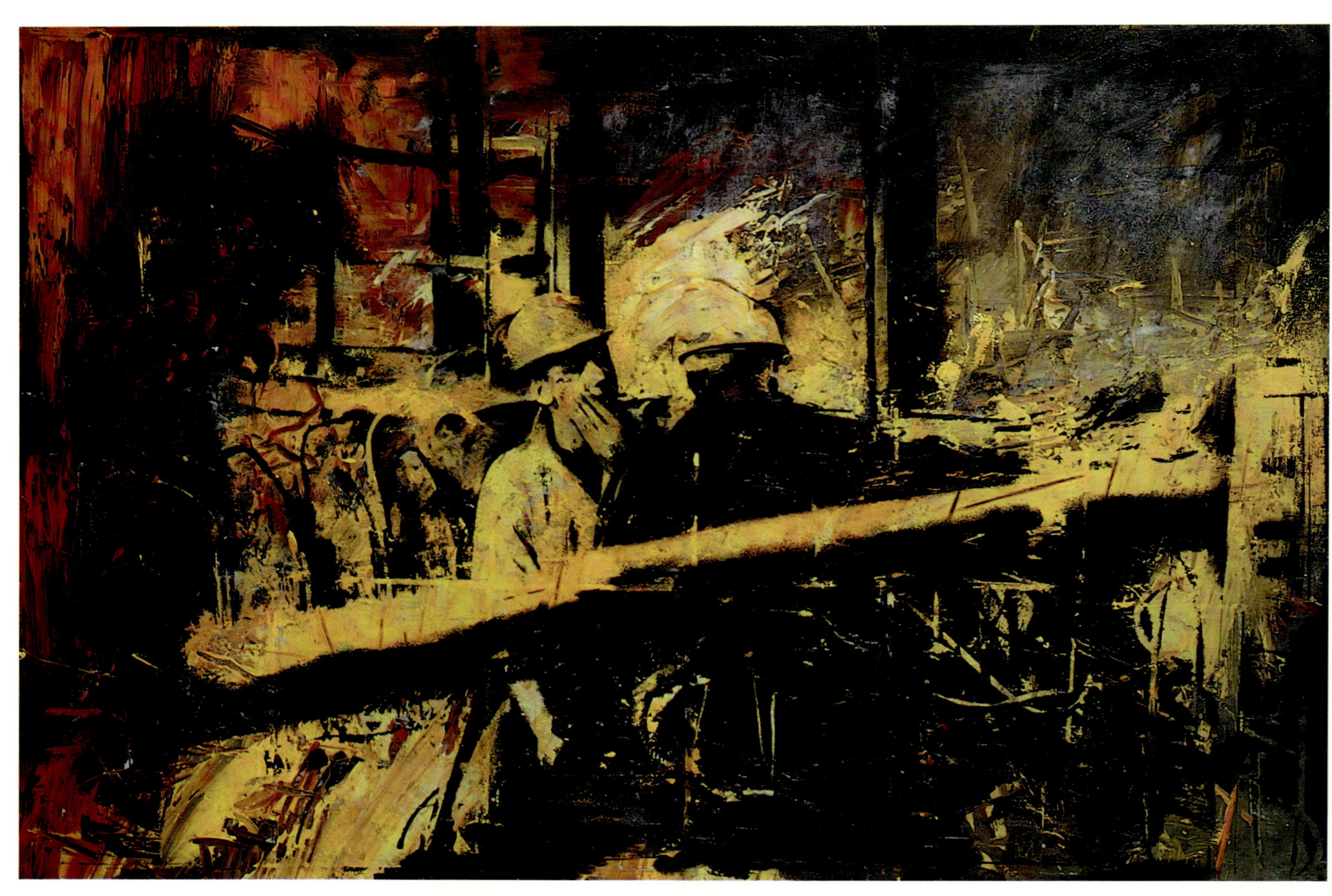

WORKERS BROADGATE (MIDDLE PANEL) 1989-90

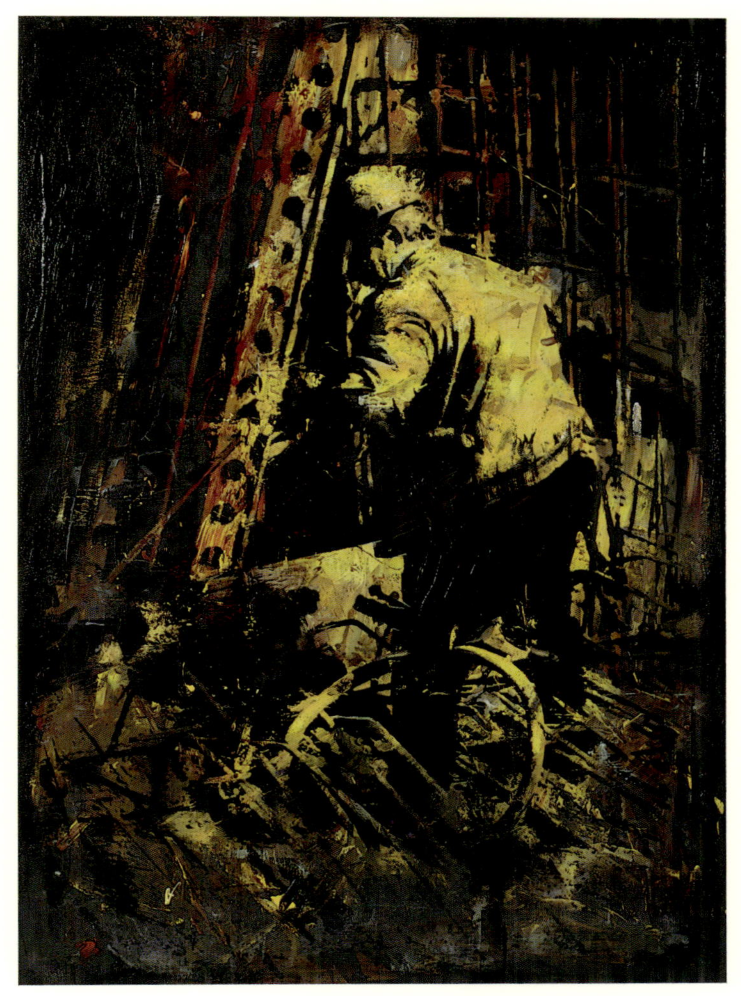

WORKERS BROADGATE (RIGHT PANEL) 1989-90

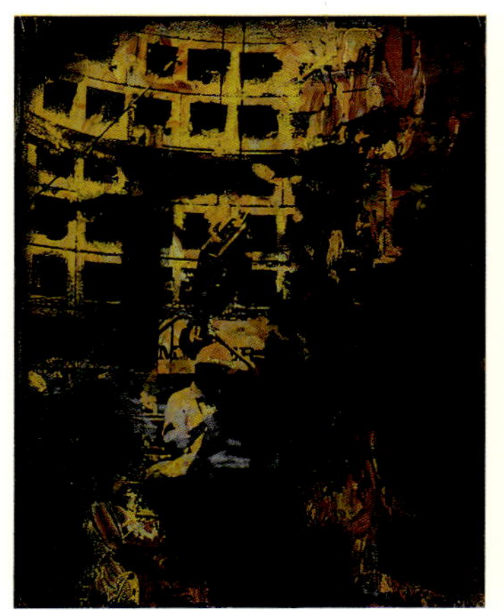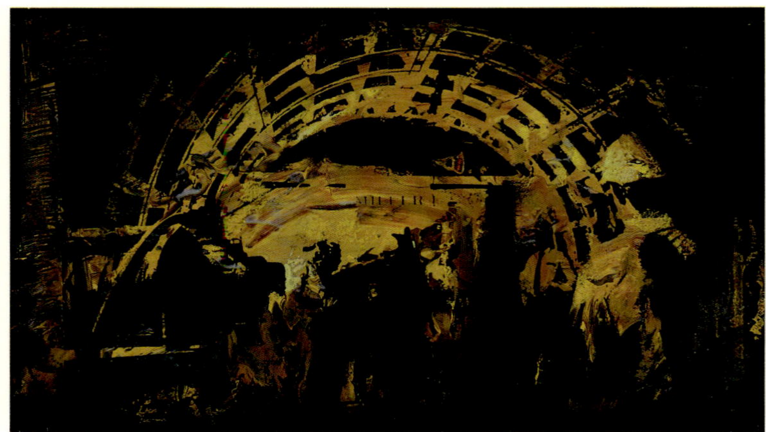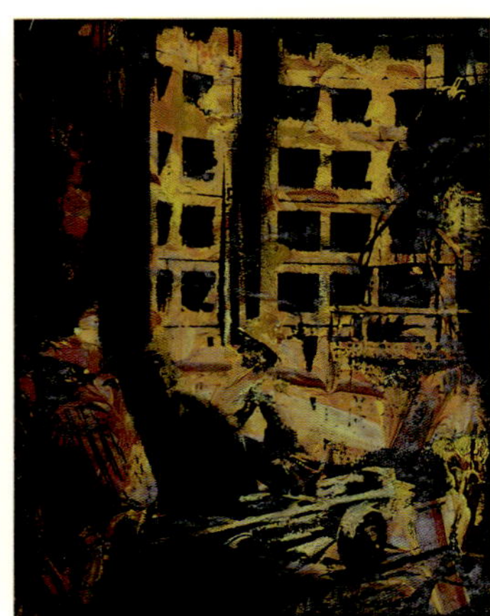

MILLERS TUNNEL (CELEBRATION OF BREAK-THROUGH 1989)

54

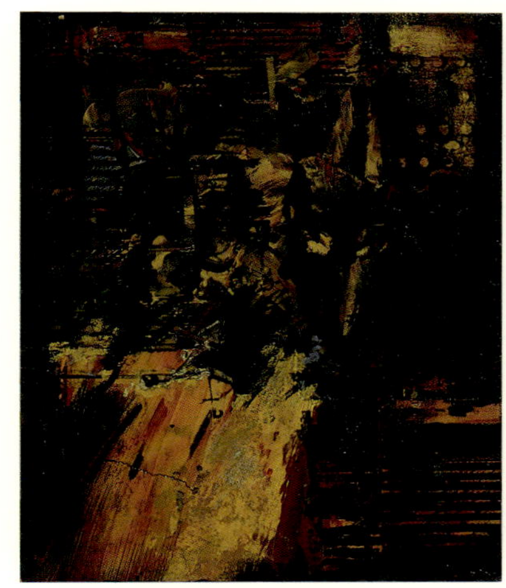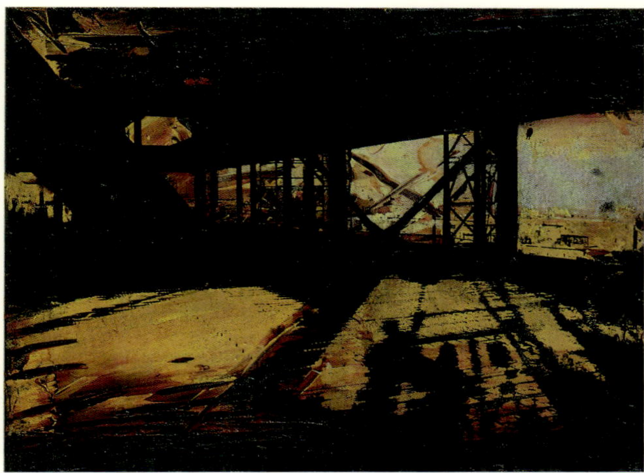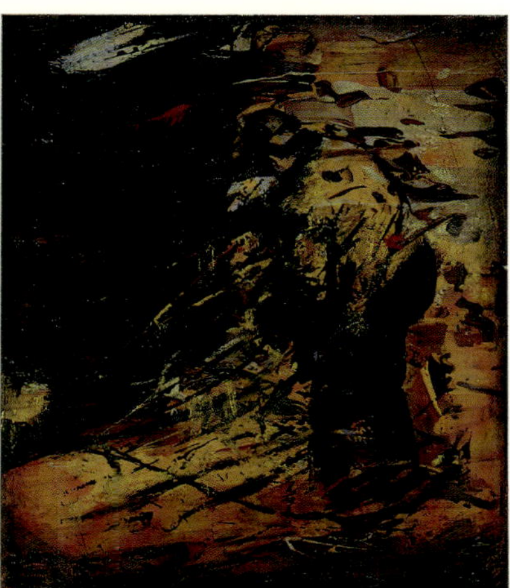

PHASE II CONSTRUCTION 1989

55

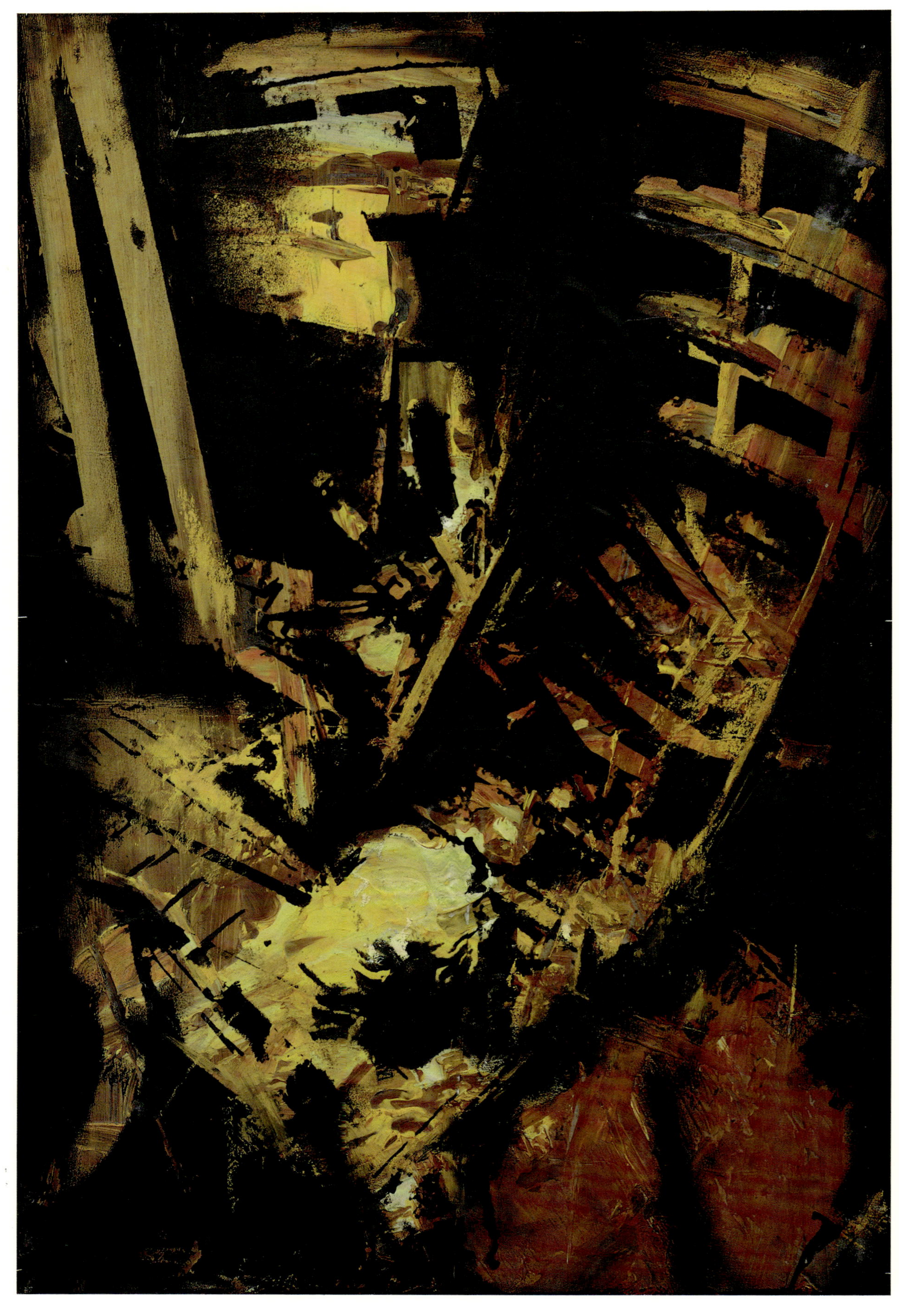

MILLERS TUNNEL (VS) I 1989

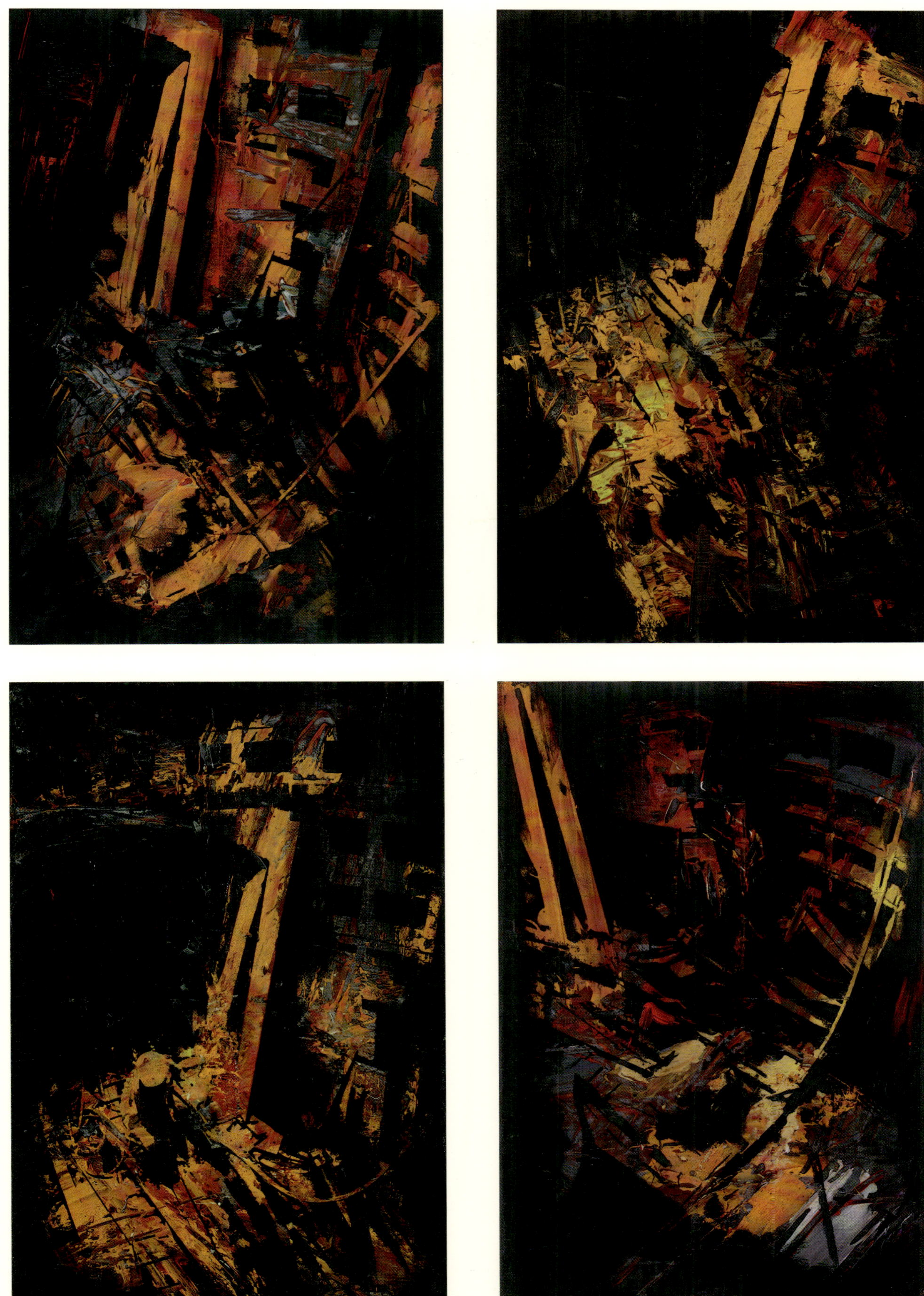

MILLERS TUNNEL I 1990   MILLERS TUNNEL IV 1990

MILLERS TUNNEL V 1990   MILLERS TUNNEL III 1990

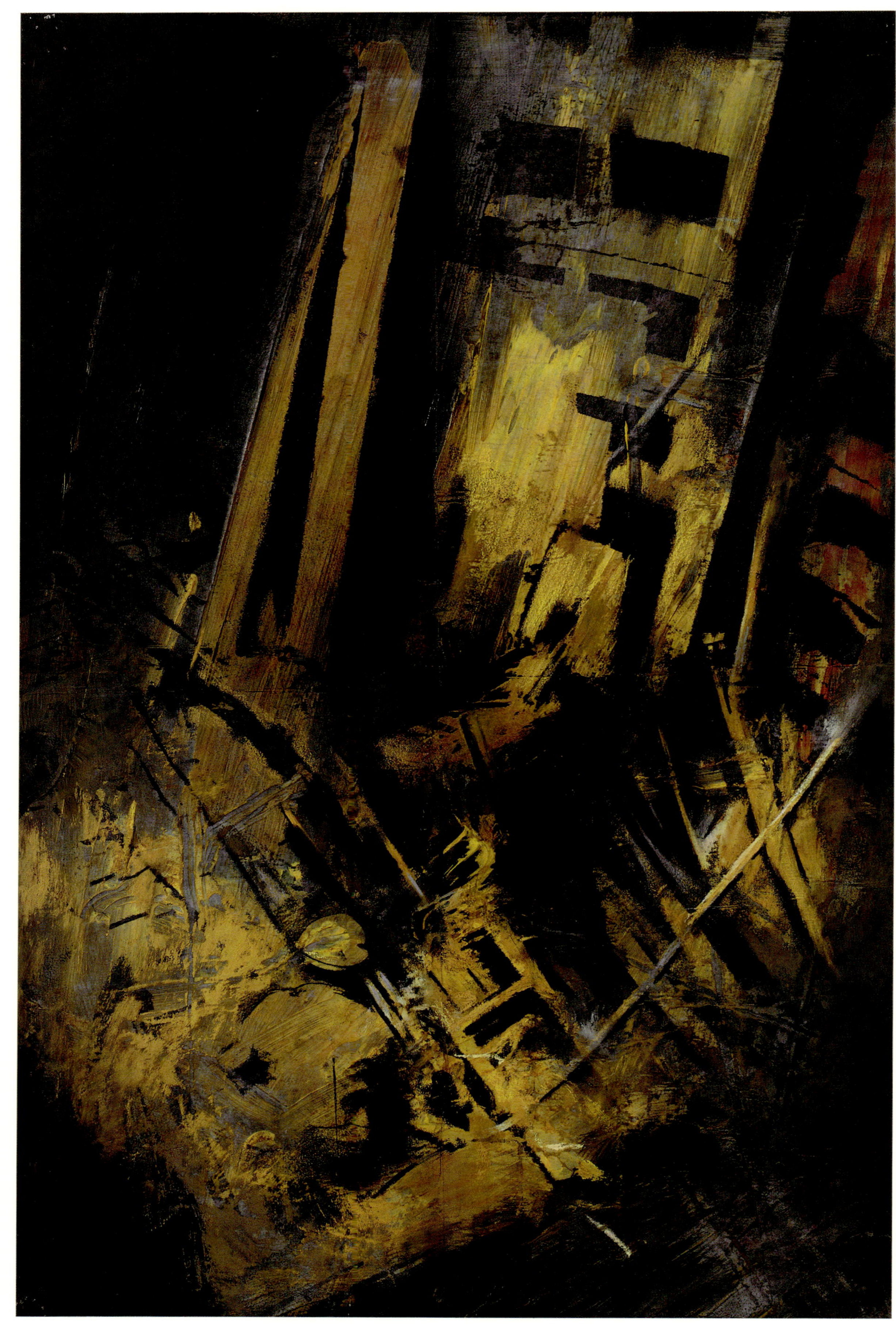

MILLERS TUNNEL (VS) II 1989

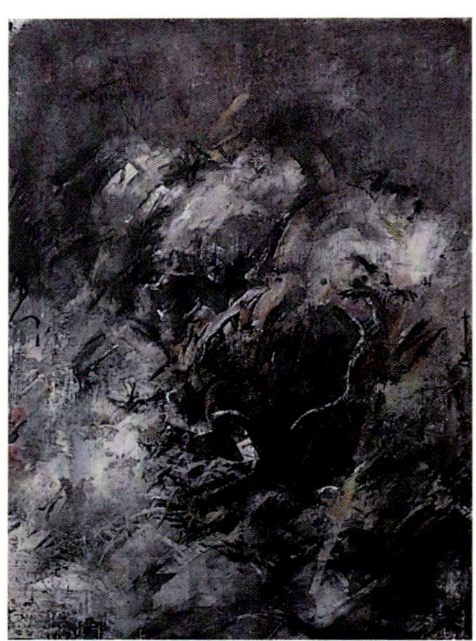

Still-life – Skulls 1980

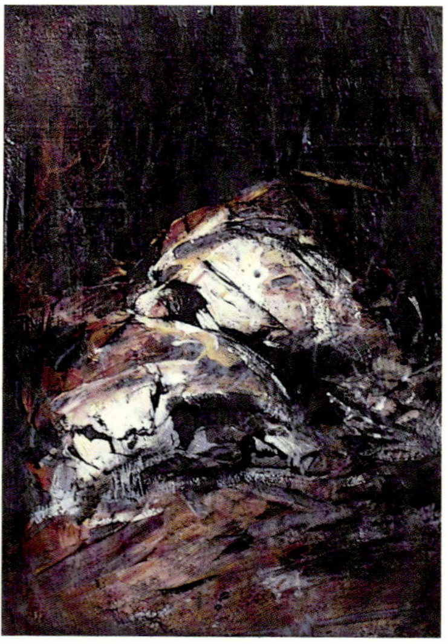

Still-life – Fowl 1982

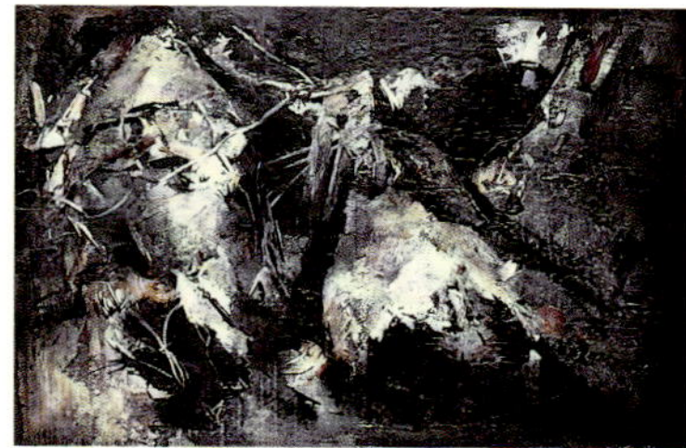

From Anticiana 1982

1946   Born Leeds, Yorkshire

1963-65   Studied at Harrogate School of Art.

1965-68
Studied at Hornsey College of Art. In 1966 became interested in the work of Edvard Munch and went to study his painting in Oslo. Joined the sculpture department at Hornsey under Hubert Dalwood and worked part-time as his assistant.

1968
Awarded the Italian Government Scholarship. After travelling in Italy, moved to the British School at Rome (leaving in June 1970). Anthony Blunt, who was staying at the School, became an important influence. Through re-examining art of the past, Mason rejected the references to Minimal art in his sculpture and began concentrating on drawing, using sources to archeology, Rome and Latin culture. Had one-person exhibitions in Rovigo and Hamburg and showed work at the Studio d'arte Condotti 85, Rome.

1970-71
Appointed visiting lecturer at the University of Florida. Stopped making sculpture and began a series of work on paper with collage, reflecting the students' concern with the Vietnam war.

1971
Returned to London and began leasing a studio in Shoreditch which is still occupied. Began a series of pictures called 'East End Assemblage' which reflected the locality and its urban decay. Showed again in Hamburg and in 'Serpentine Graphics' in 1973.

1974
Awarded first-prize (UK) Bayer's 'Herzlandschaften International' seen in Amsterdam and tour and selected by Marina Vaizey for Critic's Choice, Arthur Tooth and Sons. Began showing East End Assemblage pictures.

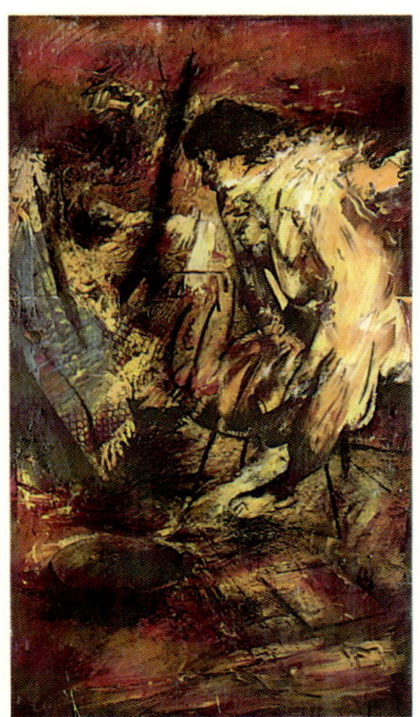

The Bowl of Emotions 1984

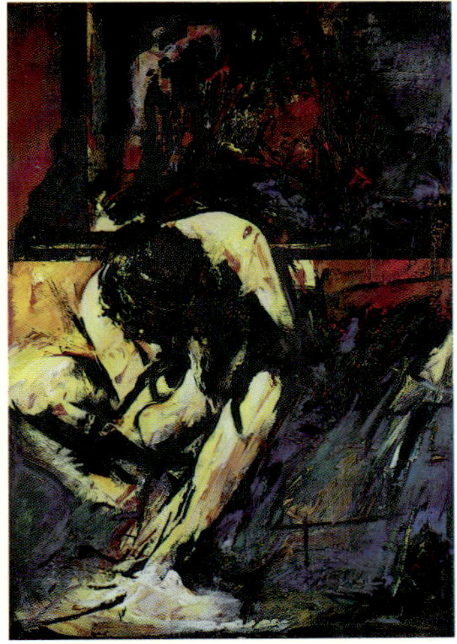

The Mask and the Stole 1986

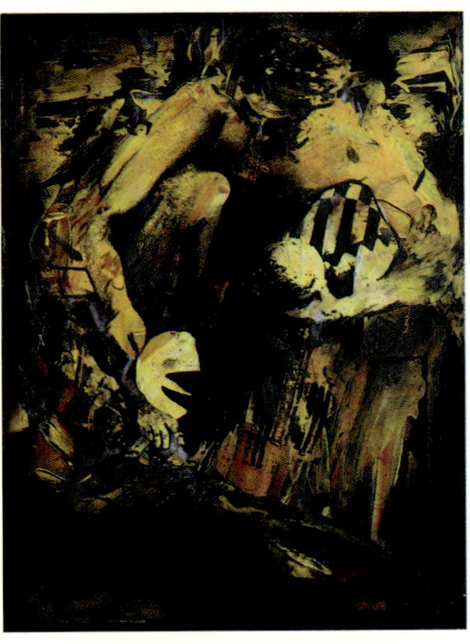

Devonshire Arms 1987

1975
Showed in 'New Work I', Hayward Gallery, London

1976
Awarded second prize, International Drawing Biennale, Middlesbrough.

1977
Awarded Arts Council Major Award and given one-person show in the Fine Art Society, University of Sheffield. Included in 'British Painting 1952-77', Royal Academy and in 'Works on Paper', Contemporary Art Society, Royal Academy and Arts Council tour.

1978
Began showing the paintings based on works from museum sources (including the Pitt Rivers Museum). One-person show at the Institute of Contemporary Arts, London.

1979
First skull paintings reflecting the loss of the artist's family (sister, brother, mother and father died during childhood of different illnesses). These were shown at the Hester van Royen Gallery.

1980-84
Continued paintings based on *nature morte*. Began showing work with the Anne Berthoud Gallery.

1983
Artist in residence at Ashby-de-la-Zouch Upper School, project based on carnival structures in Viareggio.

1984
Began series of figures and self-portraits. Catalogue 'Disclosure' with text by Sarah Kent published by the Anne Berthoud Gallery.

1986
Major one-person exhibition at the Yale Centre for British Art in New Haven, Conn. with catalogue (text by Dore Ashton) and first one-person show in New York at C.D.S. Gallery.

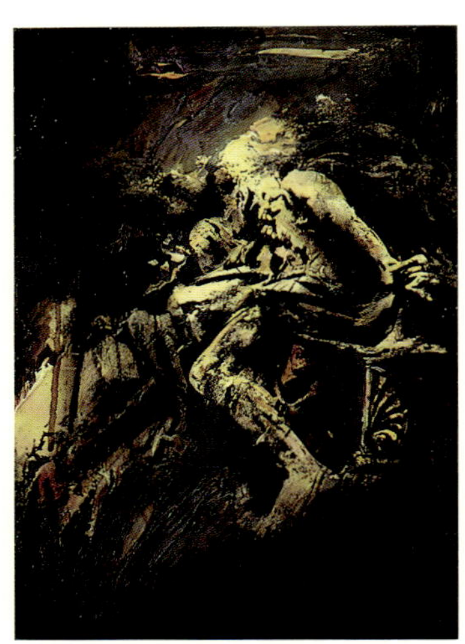

From the Borghese 1988

1988

Showed mother and child paintings, the 'Devonshire Arms' series, at the Anne Berthoud Gallery and related Yorkshire pictures at the Katzen Brown Gallery, New York. Also made paintings based on sculptures in Rome and images from Rodin's studio. Major diptych in John Moores Liverpool Exhibition 15, Walker Art Gallery. Painting of coal man. Painting acquired by the Metropolitan Museum of Art.

1989-90

In February began Broadgate pictures, spending the next twelve months drawing and documenting the buildings, workers and construction during various stages.

The portraits are of the following people, identified by name where possible, left to right, top to bottom:

PAGE 30
Stephen Cox + Stuart Lipton, Jim Colville, Godfrey Bradman; workers, Jerry.

PAGE 31
Workers, Jerry, Roy Stobart, Karen, Hal Iyengar, three men from Millers, Ray Michael;
Paul Lewis, John McLaughlin, Michael Follet.

PAGE 32
Peter Foggo, Harold Schiff, John Burcher; Peter Skead, Julie Martin, Ian Wylie, Jules Allen;
John Roukis, Harry Thomas, Shortridge, Patrick Robinson; David Blackburn, Bruce Graham,
Millers' miner.

PAGE 33
Peter Rogers, worker, Alan Etherington, Roger Kallman; Peter Kershaw, Ian Macpherson,
Bruce Vickers, Alan Dorman; Gary Hart, Lenny, Barney, worker; Peter Wynne-Rees,
Shen Adam, Andy, Jerry.

PAGE 34
John Caudle, Mick, worker, Stan George; Mike Studley, Alan Schactman, Kate Williamson,
Allan Davies, Richard Halpern; Jeff Riemer, Eugene Doyle, Howard Day, Peter,
Clive Winkler; Steve Anderson, Ann Minogue, two colleagues, Millers' man; Bill Knight,
Mick, Pat Scutt, worker.

PAGE 35
Paul Walters, Mark, Michael Cassidy; Dick Merrigan; Terry Heath, John Gosling;
Fiona Revett, Bert Coe, Monty.

PAGE 36
Worker, Mick Mannion, Jerry, Alan Smith, Tom Fridstein, Billy.

PAGE 37
Freida Davidson, Christine Jones, Bovis team.

Unless listed the works were part of the commission or are property of the artist:
Pg. 16 & 17, Private Collection; pg 19, top, Private Collection; pg. 20, Paul Lewis; pg. 21,
Private Collection; pg. 29 – top, Eric Parry; pg. 38, Skidmore, Owings and Merrill; pg 40,
Private Collection; pg 41 – bottom, U.C.A.T.T.; pg. 43, Atlantis Paper Company; pg. 44,
Private Collection; pg. 54, Private Collection; pg. 56, Seward Kennedy; pg. 57 – top left,
Private Collection, USA; pg. 58, Seward Kennedy.